THE SYMBOLS OF RELIGIOUS FAITH

By the same author

Religious Faith, Language, and Knowledge
Faith and Moral Authority

The Symbols of Religious Faith

(A Preface to an Understanding of the Nature of Religion)

by

BEN KIMPEL

Professor of Philosophy, Drew University

PHILOSOPHICAL LIBRARY
New York

COPYRIGHT, 1954, BY PHILOSOPHICAL LIBRARY, INC.
15 EAST 40TH STREET, NEW YORK 16, N.Y.

All rights reserved

PRINTED IN THE UNITED STATES OF AMERICA

To my friend

MARIE HESSE SEELEY

Preface

Just as "human" refers to a Congo Pygmy as well as to the most gifted of modern artists and scientists, so "religious life" refers to the earnest efforts of Congo Pygmy and modern men alike to acknowledge their final dependence when confronted by their ultimate insufficiency. The most enlightened of modern men, for example, are aware of the limits of their intelligence and skill in the hour they finally part with someone they love. In such an hour, the most intelligent of them is confronted by the same fact of his helplessness as is the most culturally impoverished person in a primitive society.

Man's awareness of his helplessness when confronted by the limits of his resources is not peculiar to a particular type of culture. What is peculiar to a particular type of culture is what man does to acknowledge his helplessness. The sense of total helplessness and the awareness of utter insufficiency are features of some hours in all human life, and occur wherever men live. They are neither matters of his ignorance, nor matters of his intelligence. They are inevitable in his nature, since he is incapable of controlling all that is essential to the fulfillment of his needs. Wherever human beings live, they therefore suffer for the same reason—suffer for the reason that what they most want, they cannot always control; what they most cherish, they must also relinquish.

Man's frequent inability to fulfill his most urgent needs is a feature of primitive life just as it is a feature of civilized life. Cultural differences among men are superficial when individuals are confronted with the elemental crises of life—hunger and thirst, sickness and suffering, annihilation of one's home and family by the destructive forces of nature. Men are helpless not only when confronted by the violence of nature in earthquake, avalanches of snow, torrents of rain, tidal waves, tornadoes, and hurricanes, but also when confronted by the brevity of life and the inevitability of death. All of these crises are moments in life in which men are made aware that what they most earnestly desire, they cannot completely control.

When men become aware that even their own resources are not ultimately within their control, and that all they possess may in a moment be taken from them, then, and only then, are they fully prepared to understand their status as ultimately dependent. Such an understanding is not a projection of man's insufficiency. It is an understanding of his actual nature.

A recognition of his final helplessness, and so of his ultimate dependence, is one element in man's enlightened inventory of his life. His inability to hold on to his own possessions, secure as he may believe them to be, is one fact with which every person is confronted when he is freed from the delusions of ignorance, which encourage him to depend upon what is not dependable, and to trust what is not worthy of his trusting. Man's awareness of his final helplessness is, therefore, one mark of his enlightenment. Insofar as he understands that he is not the final determiner of what he possesses, and of what he most values, he is informed of at least one aspect of his nature.

Although such understanding is essential to religious life, religious life is not merely an understanding of man's dependent nature. Essential also to religious life is the faith that there is an ultimate reality transcendent of human life and the physical world, and it is to this reality that a religious individual turns, confident that it is capable of contributing to his life what he cannot possess without it. Religious life, therefore, is not merely man's feeling of dependence—even his complete dependence: It is turning from his incompleteness to a reality which is transcendent of his incompleteness.

Yet, unless man believes there is a reality transcendent of his life, he would not turn beyond his life. It is, therefore, impossible to analyze religious life adequately without taking into account more than feeling. Although feeling is an element in religious life, it is not the only element in religious life. Religious life is an orienting of human life to a reality transcendent of human life and the physical world. It is into relation with this reality that religious life endeavors to enter, and whatever is done by religious people throughout the earth expresses what they regard as appropriate for orienting themselves to this reality. The means differ by which people of diverse cultures endeavor to relate themselves to such a reality, but underlying all of these means is one fundamental motive. It is to direct life to a reality which is trusted as human possessions and the physical world are not.

A symbol is any man-made device whose primary function is to refer beyond itself, and a religiously significant symbol is one which directs man's attention to a reality upon which he acknowledges his final dependence, which is transcendent of human life and the physical world. Just which symbolic devices are essential to religious life can be decided only by religious individuals themselves, since a symbol which is needed by an individual to refer to the reality upon which he acknowledges his final dependence is essential to his religious life. Turning from himself to acknowledge his dependence upon a reality he trusts for its dependability is a religious act, and all that is included in his efforts to acknowledge his relation to the reality he reveres as pre-eminently worthy of his trust is his religion.

Although the motive in religious life is to become oriented to a reality which is dependable as human life and the physical world are not, yet, in man's religious motivation he may cling to a symbol as if it were the most cherished of all realities. But the fact that in an hour of utmost need men cling to symbols as if they were the ultimate source of help does not itself justify any disparagement of such behavior as idolatry, in distinction to religious worship. Man's attitude toward an object which may ordinarily function as a symbol, directing him to a reality beyond it, is, in an hour of crisis, not easily detached from the source of help to which he turns. It is for this reason that even religious individuals, fully aware that a symbol is not the ultimate source of help, nevertheless, cling to it as if it were. The loss of distance between a symbol and a symbolized reality is understandable, and forgivable, when, during a crisis in life, man's dependence is so complete that even a symbol is a source of reassurance. But one test of religious faith is trusting the ultimate reality to which religious symbols refer, and not being tempted to trust the symbol. A failure, however, to preserve a distinction between a symbol and a reality to which it refers is a common occurrence in human life. Since a religiously significant symbol refers to a reality of supreme significance, the symbol itself is easily thought of as having supreme significance. It is, therefore, within this precarious margin of distinction between a symbol and a reality transcendent of it that the entire development of religious symbolism in human history takes place. This study undertakes an analysis of this phenomenon, and therefore may be looked upon as a preface to an understanding of the nature of religion.

I should like to acknowledge my indebtedness to my assistant, Marjorie B. Chambers, Senior Scholar in Philosophy, for correcting and typing the manuscript, and for reading the proofs.

Drew University
Madison, New Jersey. B.K.

TABLE OF CONTENTS

CHAPTER		PAGE
I.	The Problem of Defining Religion	1
II.	Religious Life	31
III.	The Metaphysic of Religious Life	65
IV.	The Symbols of Religious Metaphysics	97
V.	The Religious Interpretation of Symbols	132
VI.	Dependence on the Symbol	160
	References	185
	Index	193

THE SYMBOLS OF RELIGIOUS FAITH

Chapter One

THE PROBLEM OF DEFINING RELIGION

1. *Religion is often discussed even when the term "religion" is not clearly defined*

Some maintain that "religion" cannot be defined. This point of view is taken by those who look upon religion as something unique to an individual. Whatever is unique is single in kind; whereas a definition is an analysis of a type, or of a class. When religion, therefore, is regarded as unique, it follows that it cannot be defined.

That an individual's religion is a unique aspect of his life need not be questioned. In fact, any sustained effort even to interpret the nature of religion expresses an individual's belief that religion is of unique significance in his life. But because it is of such importance, it does not follow that what is of religious significance is unique to an individual in the sense that he, and he alone, can be acquainted with it. If one religious individual were to share nothing in common with another religious individual, no discussion about religious life would be possible. Even those who maintain that an individual's religious life is unique hesitate to conclude that religion cannot be discussed; yet it cannot be discussed intelligently if the sense of the term "religion" is peculiar to each individual who uses the term.

An individual's religious life is his own, and so is as unique as he himself is. But individuals may be unique and yet share certain features of their lives in common with others. The very use of proper names presupposes that one individual is distinguishable from another without being so radically unlike another that he has nothing in common with him. All of this may be admitted, without also maintaining that because individuals are unique they have nothing in common with each other. Every person is a human being insofar as he shares with others the essential features of "human" life. Yet each person is *an* individual human being because he is distinct from every other human being.

The emphasis upon the uniqueness of individuals is a common point of view. The widespread popularity of philosophies of existence, or existentialisms, indicates something of the number of people who find this point of view cogent. When, however, this point of view is taken, and one also proposes to speak about religious life as a type of experience, he is faced with a problem of defending his procedure against a charge of inconsistency. One exponent of this modern philosophy declares that individuals who "apprehend life . . . as a gift" are "naturally religious beings."[1] In speaking about an individual as religious, this philosopher obviously assumes that religious life in one sense is not unique to an individual. An individual's religion cannot be peculiar to himself to the extent that he is one example of a class of "religious beings."

But philosophers who most stress the unique nature of religious life often emphasize what is not unique to religion. An individual may "apprehend life . . . as a gift," and yet not be religious. Epicurus, the Greek philosopher, for example, was grateful for life, but certainly no one would regard him as religious. An essential part of his philosophy consists of a repudiation of every belief conventionally classified as religious. A conventional definition of religion includes an individual's acknowledgment of his relationship to a reality other than his own life, other than the lives of all men, and other than the physical world itself. But it was such a reference beyond life and beyond the physical world which Epicurus repudiated. Hence, if the term "religion" is to be inclusive of the naturalistic hedonism of Epicurus, it becomes a meaningless term, without value for either philosophical or historical studies which undertake to interpret religion as a type of human life distinguishable from other types of life. In stressing the individual nature of religion, the French existentialist,

Marcel, regards religion as an attitude toward life, without any reference beyond life itself. But a preoccupation with life has never been characteristic of any major religion of the world. To define religion as gratitude for life is simply to ignore an essential feature of religious life.

Intelligent discussion presupposes that there is some agreement about terms, and to use terms without any resemblance whatsoever to their customary meanings is to make intelligent discussion impossible. A discussion is fruitful only when it contributes to an understanding of the nature of religion as a type of human life which is distinguishable from other types of life. Such an understanding is the goal of any serious interpretation of religious life. Yet, before religious life can be distinguished from what is not essential to religious life, one must have some clear idea of the nature of religion. Such a definition is a fundamental condition for directing any interpretation of religion as a type of life.

Some of the most nebulous ideas about the nature of religion may be found even among scholars whose special field of study is religion. It would, for example, be difficult to use the term "religious" in a more diffuse manner than it is used by one of the foremost scholars of Chinese religions, who declares that "there is . . . something of religious comfort in having a scholar in the family."[2] The association of the term "religious" with an experience such as "comfort" makes one wonder just what specifically is the sense of this term. In speaking about practices in the Meditation Hall of Zen Buddhist monasteries in Japan, an equally celebrated authority says that the monks "work just as hard as ordinary labourers, perhaps harder, because to work so is their religion." And again, he says, "The rule is that each monk should eat up all that is served him, 'gathering up the fragments that remain'; for that is their religion."[3] A glance at these statements is enough to make one aware that the term "religion" is used in different senses. One use implies that hard work is religion, or essential to it, and the other that an economic use of food is religion, or is at least essential to it. But if hard work and the saving of food are essential to a Zen Buddhist religion, one naturally asks the question, "Why are these features characteristic of any religion?"—even Zen Buddhism.

One cannot regard any aspect of life as religiously significant without first having some definition of the term "religion." Religion cannot be defined as hard work, even by monks in a monastery, without raising the question, "Why is work religiously significant?" If work has religious significance in a monastery, one asks further, "Why doesn't it have religious significance outside of a monastery?" But in classifying all work, or even just earnest, hard work, as religious, one simply increases the synonyms for work, and thereby ignores any uniqueness of religion as a type of life.

A failure to distinguish an unessential element in religious life from the essential nature of religious life accounts for the vague way in which the term "religion" is so frequently used. That religion has something to do with life almost goes without saying, but the failure to distinguish religious life from life which is not specifically religious is a consequence of using the term "religion" in an indiscriminate manner. And it is used indiscriminately whenever it is not clearly defined.

2. *An adequate definition of religion is an understanding of a type of human life*

A requisite for any serious study of religion is a definition of the term "religion." But even before this term can be defined, one is confronted with the logically prior problem of clarifying the sense of a definition. In other words, "definition" must itself be defined before one can understand the real problem of defining the term "religion."

A definition is an assignment of a sense to a term. According to this point of view, any term may be used with any sense, provided individuals engaged in discussions in which defined terms are used are clearly aware of the assigned senses of the terms. Since the function of a definition is to inform individuals of the sense of terms, it is easy to see how the view arises that definitions are simply agreements on the way terms are used in discussions. When any meaning agreed upon is the definition of a term it follows that terms may be defined as individuals choose to define them. This procedure is certainly a sound rule for some discussions, but it may be pointed out that in other discussions it is not a helpful method. When terms have acquired a conventional, or traditional, sense, it is a handicap in communication to ignore these meanings and use arbitrary definitions for such terms.

The term "religion" is one language symbol whose sense is not an arbitrary decision. It refers to all that men do to take into account a reality upon which they believe they are ultimately dependent for all that is of utmost significance in their lives. Diverse as are the goods in human history which have been regarded as of utmost significance, all men who have seriously endeavored to acknowledge their dependence upon an ultimate reality for such goods share in common a belief, and a basic type of acting. Corn, for example, was of utmost importance for the Navaho Indians who were the forefathers of the present Navahos living in New Mexico, Arizona, and Utah. Aware of their dependence upon its availability, the Navaho Indians were religious in what they did to acknowledge their dependence upon a reality they believed had control over the corn which was essential to their lives. Their acknowledgment that the corn which was necessary for their lives depended in turn upon a reality which determined its supply is a reference beyond their lives, and beyond their resources. Such acknowledgments of the limits of human resources and of dependence upon a reality other than human resources are basic to every religious act. Religious acts are what men do to acknowledge their relation to a reality upon which they believe they are ultimately dependent for all they cherish. Food is indispensable for every man's life, but only religious men acknowledge their dependence upon a reality which ultimately has control over the availability of their food.

A history of religion would consist of a record of all that men have done to acknowledge their ultimate dependence upon a reality to which they are indebted for its contribution to their lives. Since the term "religion" refers to historical data, it should not be used more arbitrarily than other terms which designate historical data. It designates that aspect of human life which is distinguishable from other aspects of human life by what men do to acknowledge their dependence upon a reality believed to have ultimate significance in their lives. All that men do to acknowledge such dependence must, therefore, be taken into account in a definition of religion.

Only those efforts are religious by which men earnestly endeavor to relate themselves to an ultimately significant reality upon which they acknowledge their dependence. This qualification of a reality as that which is regarded as ultimately significant delimits the scope of religion to those efforts alone which take into account one type of reality. Although corn for the Navaho Indian was of supreme importance in his life, a religious Navaho did not acknowledge corn as an ultimate reality. Corn grows only under suitable conditions. It is a reality more ultimate than these conditions which had religious significance for the Navaho, and it is this reality with which he was supremely concerned. His corn rites constituted his attempt to acknowledge this reality for its ultimate importance in his life.

Any attempt to interpret the underlying motive of the Navaho corn rites thus involves an understanding of the Navaho religion, and such an understanding is as much a "scientific" study as is any other anthropological investigation. This understanding presupposes a distinction between what the Navaho did with his corn, and what he did to acknowledge his dependence upon a reality of more ultimate significance to him than the corn. Thus a definition of religion is not an arbitrary matter of deciding how to use a term. The real problem confronting an individual who uses the term "religion" is the taking into account of a particular type of human life which is distinguishable from other types of human life. As used in this study, "religion" designates the serious endeavor of men to acknowledge a reality they revere for its ultimate influence or control over all they value that is of utmost importance to them.

When one understands the motive which underlies the serious efforts of men to relate themselves to a reality before which they acknowledge their final dependence, he has a definition of religion. The motive underlying all religious life, irrespective of cultural peculiarities, is the earnest desire to do all that is believed to be appropriate for acknowledging man's total dependence upon an ultimate reality. An understanding of such behavior, whether it be institutional ritual or individual prayer, is a definition of religion.

Reflection upon the nature of religion is a serious effort to distinguish what is essential to religious life from what is not essential to it. Such a distinction between what is essential and what is not is one aspect of the effort to define religion. One cannot, however, understand what is essential to religious life until he has a definition of religion, and his definition of religion will be an analysis of what is fundamental to religious life. For the Ainus of Japan, millet is an essential food, without which their life is extremely difficult, if not nearly impossible. Thus it has the same significance for them that corn had for the Navaho. What is of universal religious significance is, therefore, neither millet nor corn. All men are dependent upon some food for their lives, but only when they specifically acknowledge their dependence upon the ultimate source upon which they believe the food depends, do they share in common a basic feature essential to all religious life. Essential to religious life is an acknowledgment of dependence upon an ultimate reality for the availability of what man regards as of utmost importance in his life.

An understanding of what is essential to religious life is not only a philosophical concern. It is also a "scientific" concern. A scientific study of religion is simply an informed acquaintance with one distinguishable type of human life. As Professor Wobbermin says, "The chief objective of the science of religion is to bring to light the unique meaning of the religious conviction itself."[4] One must hasten to acknowledge that only the most superficial thinking would confuse an analysis of religion with religious life. Religious life is an earnest attempt to relate oneself to a reality upon which he acknowledges his final dependence, and before which he is keenly aware of his dependent status. The pattern of such a life, however, may well be studied, and an analysis of features essential to this pattern is the objective of a philosophy of religion.

Understanding the nature of religion as a type of human adjustment is an intellectual undertaking. As such, it is a matter of an informed intelligence, and not a matter of religious experience. It is often maintained that religion can be understood only by religious individuals, when as a matter of fact an understanding of religion as a basic type of human life is all too often handicapped by a preoccupation with an interpreter's own religious life. Misunderstandings of the nature of religion consequently arise from the restriction of an interpreter to peculiarities of his own experience.

As a type of human adjustment, religion includes all that men have done to acknowledge their dependence upon a reality other than their own resources, and other than all they most cherish in life. When, for example, the Navaho Indian was confronted by the fact that the corn upon which he and his family depended for their lives was not entirely within his control, he became aware that he was not self-sufficient. When anyone is aware that his life is ultimately dependent upon factors which are transcendent of his own resources, he becomes religious by what he does to acknowledge his dependence. The Navaho Indian, as well as every other human being, can cultivate the soil in his attempt to sustain his life, but he cannot control all the conditions ultimately indispensable for the growth of his crops. After he has done all that he is able to do, he is confronted by the limits of his powers. Where his control ends, another reality assumes a pre-eminent significance because it performs a role in his life upon which he is ultimately dependent. The acknowledgment of this role, and the earnest endeavor to do all that man respectfully can to take it into account, is religious life.

The motive underlying all religious behavior is man's attempt to do what he believes is appropriate for acknowledging his dependence upon a reality ultimately determinative of what he most values in life. The Kangaroo people of Australia, for example, value the kangaroo above every other thing in life because it is their basic food, without which they cannot live. As they depend upon the kangaroo for their life, the animal assumes for them a significance greater than any other of their resources. It is what they most value as indispensable for their survival, and yet, it is not within their complete control. Whatever men most cherish which is not within their complete control alone assumes religious significance for them. With this principle as a fundamental point of view, one is able to see the basic similarity of corn for the Navahos, millet for the Ainus, and the kangaroo for one primitive people of Australia. What the Navahos, the Ainus, and the Kangaroo men of Australia do to acknowledge their dependence upon what ultimately controls the availability of their food constitutes their religion.

It is obvious that in understanding the religious life even of the most primitive of people, one becomes involved not only in an observation of rituals, but also in an interpretation of the motives for these rituals. An understanding of such motives is an understanding of their religious life. This understanding is not limited to religious individuals. It is possible to understand the nature of religious life wherever it occurs if one is capable of appreciating the basic motives underlying any instance of religious interpretation. A religious interpretation is an acknowledgment that man is dependent upon a reality more ultimate than all that he can control, and that he is therefore related to a reality transcendent of himself and of his resources. This acknowledgment underlies all that men do individually and collectively to revere the reality upon which they believe they ultimately depend.

A measure of the soundness of an individual's understanding of the nature of religion is the adequacy with which he is able to interpret the religious life of others. For such an interpretation he needs more equipment than his own religious faith. One cannot even understand what is peculiarly religious in his own life until he has some comprehension of the nature of religion as a fundamental type of human life. For such a comprehension, one needs both a respectful attitude toward cultures other than his own, and a capacity to see similarities between features in human life which may be superficially very different. It is only with such a sensitive point of view toward human life that one is able to see similarities which an individual preoccupied with his own experiences is not able to see. It is indefensible, therefore, to maintain, as Wobbermin does, that "any understanding of religious phenomena must always be based upon one's own inner religious experience,"[5] or to maintain, as Marcel does, that "I could recognize true faith in him only insofar as there was true faith in me."[6]

An essential condition for understanding religion as a type of human life is an intelligence capable of comprehending fundamental similarities. An ability to comprehend the similarity between the ritual of the Navaho and the ritual of the Kangaroo men is not a matter of an individual's own religious faith, or of his religious experience. An individual may select from among his own experiences the ones which he identifies as religious. But selecting from within one's own life what he prefers to classify as "religious" may be purely arbitrary, and have no value for enabling him to understand why some experiences, and not others, should be selected as religious.

The identification of some experiences as "religious" is a classification, and what is classified as "religious" is assumed to have features in common with all else that is classified as "religious." Any preference for one set of values, and for one set of beliefs, is a bias, and it is all too common that such a bias handicaps an individual in understanding other values and beliefs. One need only recall how a scholar such as Schaarschmidt rejected Buddhism from the classification of religion, and how others have rejected Confucianism from the category of religion. Such rejections are inevitable when selections are made in accommodation to a definition of religion which is a matter of individual preference, rather than a comprehension of features essential to a universal type of human life.

Any interpretation of religion which excludes entire cultures from the category of religion must be looked upon as insufficiently informed. A deficiency of information is, therefore, even more of a handicap to a serious study of religion than is a deficiency of religious experience in an interpreter's life. No one, however, would be likely to undertake a serious study of religion if he did not have some convictions which he regards as akin to the convictions of other religious individuals. It is one thing to have a religious life, in addition to a scholar's capacity to interpret religion as a type of human life; it is another thing to have a religious faith without the credentials of a scholar. A scholar's capacity is a requisite for a scholarly study of religious life, but not for a religious life. One may, however, have religious faith and still be unable to see any fundamental relationship between his faith and the religious faith of another. Hence, religious faith is not a sufficient, or even a necessary, condition for a philosophical analysis of religious life for the purpose of defining religion, and for testing the adequacy of the definition.

One may justifiably be impatient with the insistence that "the possibility of a religious investigator reaching a genuinely profound understanding can hold only for that religion in which he is fully at home by virtue of his own religious experience."[7] The credentials for a sympathetic study of religion are intellectual and moral, not religious. The intellectual credentials are the capacities to comprehend diverse forms of life in a single category when they are expressions of an identical motive. A moral qualification is respect for whatever men earnestly do to acknowledge their ultimate dependence, even though their efforts may be peculiar to their particular cultural contexts. An individual who is not respectful of another and of what he earnestly does within the limits of his cultural opportunities is not morally qualified to be an interpreter of religious life as a universal human type of adjustment. There is, in fact, no substitute for intellectual and moral qualifications in understanding the life of others in any of its aspects; and one aspect of human life is religious faith, and all that men do which is motivated by this faith.

3. *A definition of religion is a prerequisite for any study of religion*

It is obviously circular to maintain that a definition of religion is an essential condition for studying religion. Yet this is the case, since there would be no basis on which to classify one type of life as religious, in distinction to another which is not religious, if one did not clearly comprehend what he means by the term "religion." This fact becomes clear when scholars interpret the religious life of ancient peoples on the basis of what they assume to be evidence of "religious" practices. A glance at this method reveals its circularity. What is assumed to be of religious significance for a people is regarded as evidence for their religious life. This procedure is anything but "empirical" observation and description. It is rather a selection on the basis of an assumption. The assumption of what constitutes the religious life of a people is basic to any classification of what is assumed to be religiously significant for them, and such a classification presupposes a definition of religion.

Vast numbers of Israelite seals, for example, have been found by archeologists in Palestine. On these seals are figures of rams, lions, gazelles, and purely mythological figures, such as four-winged cobras and four-winged scarabs. When confronted with these symbols of an ancient people, a modern scholar is confronted with the problem of interpreting their significance for the people who used them. Their classification as purely ornamental is one assumption about them. Their classification as religiously significant is another assumption about them.

Every archeologist who unearths the remains of an ancient people is faced with a problem of understanding the significance of what is found. If an unearthed structure is identified as a temple, it is assumed that it has religious significance. Such an assumption, however, rests upon a definition of religion as what man does to relate himself to a reality by means of special artifacts, one of which is identifiable as a temple. If a particular structure performs this function in the life of a people, it may justifiably be classified as religiously significant. Yet the very characterization of one aspect of life in terms of what men seriously do to acknowledge a reality which they regard as worthy of special attention is an assumption about one aspect of life which is distinguishable from other aspects of life. This distinction between aspects of human life is itself an assumption about motives. To illustrate this point, one need only recall the classifications proposed by archeologists for some of the structures unearthed in earlier excavations in Palestine. A building about sixty by forty feet was excavated by Bliss and Macalister in 1899. In the court of the building were three stone pillars about six feet in height. The building was classified as a sanctuary, since it was assumed that these pillars were significant in a religious or cultic ritual. In later excavations made in 1926, comparable pillars were discovered, and they too were classified as cultic in function, on the assumption that stone pillars of this type are significant in special rites. Subsequent excavations in Palestine, however, disclosed that stone pillars were also supports for the ceilings of houses made between the ninth and sixth centuries B.C. Thus, what was once classified as a sanctuary was later reclassified as a dwelling. What is instructive about this classification, as well as about all classifications, is that classifications are interpretations, and interpretations are based on assumptions. Had Bliss and Macalister known the function of the structure they classified as a "sanctuary," they would never have placed it in the category they did. The structure was incorrectly classified because incorrectly interpreted, and the indefensible interpretation was a result of a fallacious assumption about its function.

When the specific function of any artifact is not definitely known, its classification is subject to misunderstanding. This is a fundamental principle which ought never to be lost sight of in interpreting any artifacts, whether buildings or symbols on seals. An artifact may be examined by anyone, but its classification is something very different from a mere examination, or observation. Anyone who examines the vast number of Israelite seals found in excavations made in Palestine can easily see the figures of lions, rams, bulls, griffins, gazelles. But an interpretation of their functions for the people who made them is a very different matter. This function cannot be observed. It must be assumed; and an assumption is not an observation. If it were definitely known what role these symbols performed, no mistaken classification would be made. But when their function is not definitely known, their classification must be regarded as tentative. Symbols are classified on the basis of an assumption about their significance, and yet, it is this very significance which is assumed.

The classification of symbols as significant for cultic ritual when found in buildings assumed to be cultic in function involves a double assumption. That such assumptions are not always tenable becomes evident when one knows that during certain periods of history, such as the Roman-Byzantine, symbols were used in Jewish synagogues for purely artistic purposes, and not specifically for cultic or religious use. Thus, when two symbols, physically identical, are classified as identical in function, the classification is no more accurate than the assumptions are informed. Accurate classification of symbols is a matter of the adequacy of information about their significance for the people who created them. When a symbol used in a synagogue during the Roman-Byzantine period is classified as religiously significant, the classification is open to question. The uncertainty about the soundness of the classification arises from the fact that within the very same structure, some symbols were used for decorative or artistic purposes, and others were used for religious purposes. This distinction is not a matter of observation. It is an assumption about the intended function of the symbols. When one understands the function of a symbol, he knows how to classify it. But when he does not know the specific function for which it was created, his classification cannot be more than probably defensible. The realization that his classification is tentative is an acknowledgment that it is after all only hypothetical.

To classify symbols in one category, when more than one classification is possible, is to presume to tell the people who used them what significance the symbols had for them. The problem of an archeologist is to find this out, and his method in doing so is not exhausted by the skill of his spade work.

Many rock pillars have been unearthed in archeological excavations in Palestine, and some of them have been classified as altars. But the classification of a cut-rock pillar as an altar is an assumption about its function. If such a pillar actually had been made for the purpose of performing a sacrifice intended to relate men in some special way to a reality upon which they acknowledged their ultimate dependence, then it had religious significance. But if a pillar cut from rock performed another function, its classification as an altar would obviously be open to question. That pillars were used for non-cultic, or non-ritual purposes, is an assumption made by Professor Albright. When one takes this assumption into account, any classification of cut-rock pillars in Palestine becomes problematic. An archeologist's problem is to ascertain which function a particular pillar performed for the people who made it. One such pillar in northwestern Judea, near Zorah, is regarded by Professor Albright as "of undoubted religious function," whereas "many alleged groups of *massebôth* (stone pillars), he maintains "have nothing to do with religious worship." Professor Albright's differentiation between physically comparable artifacts does not rest primarily upon observation. It rests rather upon observations made from a point of view. The point of view with which he made his observations is an assumption about the functions of such objects.

When classifications are not merely matters of observation, but of interpretation, classifications must be regarded as hypothetical. They are hypothetical because they rest upon assumptions, and when assumptions are basic to classifications, classifications must be treated cautiously. As Professor Albright points out, "a great many mistakes have been made, and stone basins . . . stone pillars, large forks, peculiar types of pottery, etc., have been interpreted without adequate ground as cultic in function."[8]

The competency of any classification of religiously significant artifacts or symbols is a matter of understanding the specific functions of such artifacts or symbols. This understanding is not something to be taken for granted. It is a goal to be achieved. A presumption about the function of a symbol may be nothing more than ignorance masquerading as assumed knowledge. No one should presume to pass definitive judgment upon the significance of any symbol used by another without understanding the function of that symbol in the life of that person. Understanding the significance of a symbol is knowing the function it performs for the individual who uses it. Such understanding is necessarily most incomplete when people who use symbols cannot also give an articulate commentary upon their specific function.

That this is the case with ancient civilizations is obvious. Many languages are yet to be deciphered, and the significance of many non-language symbols is yet to be understood. Among such non-language symbols used by ancient peoples are representations of the sun and moon. It is commonly assumed that every sun and moon representation among ancient peoples is of cultic or religious significance. Yet, according to Professor Mylonas, this assumption is open to question. His doubts about its defensibility are results of his studies of the prehistoric culture of Crete, known as the Minoan-Mycenean culture, which dates from about 3000 to about 1100 B.C. Among the symbols characteristic of this culture are sun and moon representations. But, according to him, "no evidence has yet been found proving the existence of a cult of the heavenly bodies in Minoan-Mycenean times." On the basis of this deficiency of evidence, he therefore classifies such representations of heavenly bodies as "works of art" whose artistic significance is to provide a "natural setting within which a scene was placed."

A classification of representations of heavenly bodies as "religiously significant" is an assumption about their symbolic function. If they refer to heavenly bodies for the purpose of acknowledging man's ultimate dependence upon them, they are rightly classified as religiously significant. But when representations of heavenly bodies do not perform this symbolic role, and are used specifically for the artistic enrichment of man's life, it is indefensible to classify them as religiously significant. The classification, therefore, of physically similar symbols as religiously significant presents a problem. Anyone familiar with the ancient mystery rites of Greece knows that the bull had ritual significance in the Dionysian and Eleusinian rites. On the basis of this knowledge, one might infer that the bull was venerated by the Minoans, since Minoan-Mycenaean civilization flourished in the very region out of which the mystery rites of Greece later arose. But, according to Professor Mylonas, this inference would be most incautious. He says, "as far as our evidence to date goes neither the bull nor any other animal was venerated by them."[9]

In order to know which artifact of an ancient people is to be regarded as religiously significant, and which is not, one must first learn the function which the artifacts performed for the people who made them. To classify an artifact as religiously significant when one does not know its function for the people who made it, is to take liberties which are unwarranted in any intellectually responsible study. Some classification, however, is unavoidable in any study of cultures, and therefore some assumptions must be made. Yet when an assumption is made, it is also a part of responsible scholarship to be aware of that assumption.

When the specific function of an artifact is not definitely known, two assumptions are always implicit in any classification of it as religiously significant. One assumption is that there was an aspect in the life of the people who used it which corresponds to what an interpreter regards as religious. Another assumption is that the particular artifact performed a particular function in the aspect of life which is classified as religious. The complex character of any classification in archeological studies is thus obvious. It is no less obvious that an anthropological study of a living people is also encumbered with assumptions.

The totem-animal or totem-plant is, for many primitive people, a reality upon which they have as keen a sense of dependence as any civilized person has in relation to a deity. Although a totem is the center of a type of life found among many primitive people, and is often classified as religious, it would be a mistake, according to Professor Murphy, to classify all totems as religiously significant. This qualification in a classification takes account, for example, of the role of the totem among the Bantu people, for whom "The Totem . . . is of social rather than religious significance."[10] This distinction between totems which have religious significance and those which do not have such significance presupposes information of their specific roles among primitive people.

Whatever confidence one may have in the defensibility of his classification of totems rests upon his belief that the significance of a symbol for a primitive people may be inferred from what they do in relation to it. That this is a sound principle in some cases need not be doubted. But that it is a principle which may be used as a methodological procedure without further caution is indefensible. Some primitive people are so secretive about some of their rites that an anthropologist can learn about as much of their mentality from observing what they do as an archeologist can learn of the mentality of an ancient people from their artifacts. Some primitive people do not reveal everything they believe in the rites they perform for public inspection. Hence even anthropologists, observing the practices of living primitives, cannot always be entirely confident that their classifications of symbols are as defensible as they wish they were.

An anthropologist classifies what he observes according to the categories he uses. But such categories have a significance for him which they do not necessarily have for the people he studies. When an anthropologist classifies some behavior observed among primitive people as "religious," he employs a definition of religion, and what he regards as "religion" constitutes the category according to which he classifies another person's life as religious. No anthropological study can be undertaken without a procedure involving assumptions. Yet, an anthropologist studying the Aborigines of Australia declares, "I have not attempted to define religion, and then to describe those beliefs and practices which fit the definition. I have preferred to describe . . . the Aborigines' non-material adjustment to the unseen."[11] But this procedure is based upon a definition of religion. Religion for this anthropologist is defined as "non-material adjustment to the unseen." Thus this scholar has a definition of religion without regarding it as a definition.

A religious adjustment is made when men believe in the existence of a reality upon which they acknowledge their ultimate dependence. An individual may believe in the existence of an "unseen world," however, without acknowledging his dependence upon it. A belief in an "unseen world" is characteristic of speculative philosophies, but a speculative belief about reality is very different from an earnest effort to do all that one can to acknowledge his ultimate dependence upon it. No adjustment is religious without a belief in an "unseen world," or "unseen powers or beings," but a belief in such realities is religious only when men earnestly do all they can to acknowledge their ultimate dependence upon them.

"A purely historical study of religion," is, therefore, a fiction. Any classification of elements within a culture as "religiously significant" is a selection made on the basis of a belief about the nature of religion, and such a belief is a definition of religion. A classification of objects regarded as religiously important to a people is an empirical operation, but it takes for granted the warrant for such a classification. It is just this which may not be taken for granted. The warrant for classifying any artifact, symbol, or rite, as an element in a people's religion is a problem, and to assume the warrant for a classification is to beg the question. The question with which an interpreter of the religious life of a people is faced is whether or not he understands the intended function of such artifacts. Such an understanding is an essential condition for any competent study of a religion, and this is not merely a matter of the accuracy of description. A description of whatever is classified as religiously significant for a people is informative of their religious life only when the classification is itself warranted, and it is warranted only when an interpreter selects artifacts for description which actually perform a function for a people which the interpreter assumes they perform. It is obvious that such a procedure is more than description. But because description is not the only method for studying a religion, a study of religion cannot be purely empirical. It is not purely empirical even when it proposes to be "based exclusively upon history." No actual historical study conforms to such a fictional ideal as Kaftan, the distinguished historian of religions, assumed. What Kaftan selected from a complex culture for its religious significance expressed his presupposition of the nature of religion. The circularity of his procedure is apparent. His procedure is from a point of view, and no matter how careful his observations, and no matter how accurate his descriptions, the descriptions of what he observed are no more informative of the actual religious life of a people than is his understanding of the uses of the artifacts, symbols, and rites he observes and describes.

As a historian of the earliest culture of Greece, Professor Mylonas says that "Our knowledge of that religion depends solely on the evidence obtainable from objects of art and from the remains of settlements brought to light by excavations." And yet, as he points out, all of these observed items are "subject to varied interpretation."[12] One such interpretation is that they are religiously significant. Another interpretation is that they are not, and Professor Mylonas himself doubts the "religious character" of many of these artifacts. His doubt expresses his understanding that artifacts which are physically identical may have been created to perform various functions.

Many scholars have assumed that the caves in the Pyrenees fulfilled a religious function for men of the Middle Stone Age. Professor Murphy, for example, interprets "the wealth of . . . art discovered in the caves" as a "source of light upon the religion of Palaeolithic Man." With this same assumption, another historian of religion embellishes upon the interpretation of the artifacts of this so-called Magdalenian culture. He speaks of the "mile-long subterranean cathedral with pillars, side-chapels and confessionals all complete."[13] That the caves may have been significant in Palaeolithic man's efforts to acknowledge his dependence upon a reality in relation to which the "pillars, side-chapels, and confessionals" performed a significant role, can no more confidently be affirmed than it can be dogmatically repudiated. When, however, one knows that some of the earliest symbols of animals in the so-called Stone Age may have performed a magical function to help man in his hunts, one becomes cautious in classifying any particular example of cave art as undoubtedly "religious" in function. Just which art was created to fulfill magical functions; which to fulfill religious functions; and which to delight man as artist certainly confronts any serious student with a problem.

Even if one does have a definition of religion which is plastic enough to be applied to cultures as diverse as those of the Stone Age and the twentieth century Christianity of modern metropolitan centers, he still is faced with the difficulty of knowing which objects in these diverse cultures have symbolic significance for referring to a reality upon which men acknowledge their ultimate dependence.

To illustrate this problem further one need only point out how widespread is the assumption that all utensils buried with the dead performed a single function, which was to equip the dead for a life to come. That this may have been the intended function of such mortuary deposits certainly cannot be repudiated. But such an unqualified assumption may well be questioned. It is a fact that graves classified as Neolithic "contain jars," but it is not a fact of the same empirical character that these jars "doubtless contained food for the departed."[14] That they did contain food intended to equip the dead for a life to come is an inference. It is assumed that people believed in a life to come, and so vessels buried with the dead are inferred to be equipment significant in a preparation for a life to come. This may be a warranted interpretation of all mortuary vessels, but it is after all an interpretation which rests upon an assumption for which there is no definitive empirical evidence. Modern men lay floral tributes on the graves of friends and relatives, not because they assume the flowers will be of use to them either now or in a hereafter, but because anyone who loves another wants to do something to express his affection. Flowers perform this function for modern men, and bowls of food may have had no more significance for early men. The motive for primitive men, as for us, may have been the desire to do something to express respect and affection. What little the living can do to express affection for the dead confronts man with his impotence. Wanting to do so much, and yet aware of his impotence for expressing his desires, he does what seems to him to be most worthy of the dead whom he cherishes. Primitive men may have done this by burying food and utensils. Hence, an interpretation of all burials of food as evidence that all primitive men believe in the survival of the dead would be as hasty an inference as it would be to infer that the modern practice of sending floral tributes is empirical evidence that men today believe that flowers are somehow significant in the future status of the dead. Primitive men may have believed that there is another life after death, but it is a precarious inference to conclude this from the "evidence" of artifacts. The belief that mortuary artifacts are "evidence" for any specific point of view of early men is an assumption about the functions which artifacts were intended to perform.

Murphy says that "it was a very old custom to feed (the dead) with food and drink." But a strictly historical study would have to be more empirical than this. It would have to be content with the statement that "it was a very old custom to bury food and drink" with the dead. Just what the function of such food and drink may have been for early men is a matter of conjecture, and certainly not of observation and description. After it is assumed that primitive men believe in a life to come and do what they can to equip the dead for this life, it seems defensible to interpret all mortuary offerings and utensils as evidence for a belief in another life. When it is assumed that a belief in a life to come is a universal religious conviction of mankind, it is easy to interpret whatever is done for the dead as evidence that the dead are believed to live again. But whether it is a universal belief that the dead will live again is just the problem with which a historian of early cultures is confronted.

What early men have done for the dead is often interpreted as "evidence" for their belief that there is another life. The status of such "evidence," however, is a matter for question. Professor Mylonas, for example, maintains that "we have no real evidence to prove the existence of a cult of the dead in prehistoric Greece."[15] Prehistoric men may have done much for the dead, just as some modern men do, and yet they may not have had any clearer notion of a life to come than many modern men have. Thus even what seems such "obvious" evidence for the belief in a life after death as mortuary artifacts is, after all, an interpretation of "evidence" which rests upon an assumption, the warrant for which is open to question. The extent to which this assumption may be questioned is the extent to which it is precarious to read back into "evidence" that for which one assumes it is "evidence."

What has been said about the caution which must be taken in interpreting artifacts used centuries ago may also be said about interpretations of "religious" experiences of men today. Only after it is assumed that certain behaviors have a specific significance can they be classified as "religious." But many behaviors which overtly resemble each other may express vastly different intentions. When the motivating intention of one act differs from the motivating intention of another act, the acts certainly are not in the same category. The difference between motives underlying apparently identical behaviors makes strictly empirical studies of human behavior either very superficial or downright inaccurate. This questionable procedure is basic to the famous studies made by William James in *Varieties of Religious Experience.* James proposed to observe what is essential to religious life, and on the basis of his "empirical" study derived what he assumed to be an analysis of the nature of religion. His assumption of what is religious was, of course, basic to the data he selected for its religious significance. The procedure of his so-called "empirical psychology" is as circular as is the same method in empirically "scientific" archaeological studies of religion. Underlying every classification of religious experiences, religious acts and symbols, is an assumption that such experiences, acts, and symbols share in common certain features. A strictly empirical psychology of religious experience is therefore no more possible than is a strictly empirical historical study of religion. Any historical study of religious life, just as any psychological or philosophical study of religious experience, proceeds from assumptions about religion as a distinguishable type of human life.

4. *A definition of religion is a point of view with which to interpret one type of human life*

When religion is defined as a type of human life, it is assumed that religion is not peculiar to particular cultures, but occurs in one form or another in all human cultures. This interpretation of religion is, of course, a presupposition. It is clearly an assumption about the nature of religion, both about its universality, and also about its conditioning in relation to other aspects of human culture. Although the religion of a particular people is always conditioned by factors peculiar to their culture, still, in spite of this, there is a character common to all religions which is a fundamental type of human life, and is not a function of culture. This proposal to study religion as one type of human life distinguishable from other types of human life is an assumption about religion as a pattern of adjustment which is not peculiar to particular cultures.

If beliefs or practices which are peculiar to one culture were essential features of religion, religion could not defensibly be defined as a universal human phenomenon. A premise basic to this study is that religion is a universal type of human life. This premise, therefore, is a presupposition constituting a point of view with which both human cultures and also religion are interpreted.

If, for example, a Moslem were to define "true religion" as all that is included in the teachings of Mohammed about what men ought to do for acknowledging their dependence upon Allah, he would necessarily reject non-Islamic beliefs and practices from the category of what is essential to religion. The evaluation of his faith as "true religion" implies a definition of religion in terms peculiar to his own faith, that "there is no God but Allah, and Mohammed is His prophet." That every non-Moslem would regard this procedure as arbitrary almost goes without saying. Its arbitrary character, however, would not be so apparent to a Moslem. It would, in fact, be no more apparent to him than would a definition of religion by a Christian be regarded as arbitrary when expressed in terms of faith in Christ. The essence of a Christian's faith is his acknowledged dependence upon Christ. One would not even be a Christian if the supreme significance of Christ were not central to his religious life. One likewise would not be a Moslem if the teachings of Mohammed were not the final scriptural authority for his religious life. All of this may be admitted, and yet the very acknowledgment by a Moslem that it is Mohammed, and no other prophet, who has outlined all that men ought to do in their relation to God makes one person a member of Islam rather than a member of some other religion. This acknowledgment, however, of the Moslem's dependence upon the teachings of the Prophet for affirming allegiance to God and loyalty to his Law is an act of a religious life. The fact that such a religious act, for a Moslem, is in terms of what he regards as his supreme obligation ought not to blind an intelligent person to the similarity of a Moslem's faith and his own, when his own faith is also an acknowledgment of his final dependence upon a reality of supreme significance over every other reality, because he recognizes it to be the ultimate determiner of all that he most cherishes.

The proposal that a definition of religion should not be peculiar to the faith of a Moslem, or to the faith of a Christian, is itself a presupposition about the nature of religion. Only when it is assumed that religion can be analyzed in terms which are not peculiar to a particular culture, is it also assumed that religion is not a possession of one people. But this point of view is an assumption about religion. It is an assumption that although religious faiths are expressed in forms peculiar to particular cultures, there are, nevertheless, features common to diverse religious faiths which are not functions of any one culture.

When, however, the religion of one people is regarded as

the norm of what every other people should believe and do, it is simply impossible to regard religion as a fundamental type of human life, and so as a universal aspect of human life, irrespective of cultural peculiarities. The belief that there is one, and only one, "true" faith is even incompatible with the belief that an individual can profit in his own religious life by intelligently understanding the religious life of others. Such an understanding is impossible for an individual who is dogmatically confident that he knows all that can be known about what is worthy of man in acknowledging his dependence upon an ultimate reality.

Without presuppositions, one cannot interpret the relations between various religions. One makes at least two assumptions, for example, if he maintains that the faith of Israel is the beginning of a "revelation" which culminated in the Christian faith. One is that there is a continuity of two distinguishable religions, and the other is that the continuity can be accounted for not by cultural accidents, but by the intention of God to link one culture with another, both of which therefore are favored above all others. That this is a defensible point of view for interpreting the religion of Israel and Christianity is a presupposition, and it is on the basis of this presupposition that an individual finds features in common to both religions which he would not notice without it. Without an assumption of the continuity of these religions, there would be no basis even for comparing what they have in common. The assumption that these two, of all the religions of the world, have an affinity on the basis of a revelation unique to them is a point of view which may give comfort, but it certainly does not provide a helpful premise for understanding the religious life of all who are not included in this "favored" Jewish-Christian tradition.

Every person with a religious faith has a point of view which is conditioned by some culture, and this implies that his point of view in interpreting religions is also culturally conditioned. It is therefore only with earnest endeavor that an individual can have a living faith conditioned by one culture, and yet have a capacity to study respectfully other religions with a desire to discover in them what may enrich his own religious life. Anyone who already believes that what he is and what he does are all that can enter into the definition of religion is, of course, spiritually and intellectually incompetent to undertake any understanding study of religion as a universal human phenomenon.

When one studies the anthropological data of primitive cultures in order to understand what is common to his religious life and to primitive religious life, he has a point of view which could not be maintained by another who presumes that religion is unique to civilized life. The distinction between civilized cultures and primitive cultures is a defensible procedure in classifying cultures, but such classification is after all only a distinction between cultures. When one assumes that religion is a fundamental type of human adjustment, he also assumes that religion is not strictly a cultural characteristic. This analysis of religion rests upon the assumption that in spite of cultural peculiarities which differentiate one religion from another, there are essential features which culturally different religions have in common. Thus one type of life of the most primitive of peoples may be classified in the same category as a type of life of the most civilized of peoples.

The identification of one type of a primitive people's life with one type of a civilized people's life does not imply that there are no fundamental distinctions between primitive and civilized life. Primitive life is distinguishable from civilized life by a thousand traits. Yet, insofar as both are classifiable as "human," one assumes that they have some traits in common.

Human nature is one in its dependence upon all the elementary conditions requisite for life itself. No one, regardless of his culture, can live without food. Irrespective of their culture, individuals soon became aware of their dependence upon food. Such an awareness of dependence is an element in religious life, however, only when men acknowledge that there is a reality other than their food upon which they are ultimately dependent for its availability. This distinction between dependence upon food, and dependence upon a reality acknowledged to be ultimately determinative of its availability, is essential to religious life. All human life is dependent upon food. But only that life which acknowledges its dependence upon a reality ultimately controlling the availability of its food interprets its food from a religious point of view.

The point of view basic to religious life is the acknowledgment of dependence upon an ultimate reality. Food is not an ultimate reality. The very fluctuations in its supply confront primitive and civilized man alike with the fact that it is not completely within his own control. Man's acknowledgment that the food which is an essential condition for his life is ultimately contingent upon a reality other than his resources likewise accounts for his acknowledgment that he too is ultimately dependent upon this same reality. Thus food, which is essential for man's life, constitutes one of the occasions for his religious acknowledgment of his dependence, not upon the food, but upon a reality believed to be ultimately significant in making food available.

The chief item of diet for the Witchetty Grub Eaters of Central Australia is the witchetty grub. Hence it is not surprising that this grub should be the most significant reality in their life, since without it they cannot survive. Their dependence upon the grub for their survival consequently assumes religious significance in what they do to acknowledge their dependence upon a reality which they believe controls its supply. The grub totem is a symbol of their belief that the grub itself, upon which they depend for life, is contingent upon a reality which controls its availability. An awareness of dependence upon the grub as an essential food is thus indirectly an acknowledgment of dependence upon whatever is significant in conditioning its supply for them. Hence this most primitive of people regard the grub as a sign, because it directs their attention beyond the grub itself to a reality which they believe ultimately controls it.

This reference beyond an essential item in man's life to a reality believed to be ultimately in control of it is a fundamental feature of all religious life. Religious life is an acknowledgment of dependence upon a reality other than human resources, and other than everything which man possesses. The primitive Australian, for example, possesses the grub which he has gathered, but he does not possess the factors which make such grubs available for his gathering. From the point of view of a religious individual, possessions are not completely man's own, but are contingent. An acknowledgment of the contingency of all human possessions is an element in a religious interpretation. Essential to religious life is the acknowledgment that although men possess the food which they grow or gather, they do not control the conditions which make its growth possible. This awareness of the limits of human abilities becomes a religious acknowledgment of dependence when men do what they can to take into account the reality upon which they believe they are ultimately dependent.

The Ainus, for example, in acknowledging the indispensability of millet for their life, offer thanksgiving to millet "as to a personal being." This expression of gratitude to the millet, however, would not be religiously significant were they preoccupied with the millet as a food. The millet itself would not be religiously significant for them, dependent as they are upon its availability, if they did not make a distinction between it as cereal which they possess, and a reality other than it which they do not possess, but upon which they acknowledge their final dependence. Hence it is their respectful regard for a "power" which ultimately controls the millet which is the religious feature of their behavior.

This simple distinction, obvious as it may be, is nevertheless a distinction basic to all religious life. Religious life includes all that men do to acknowledge their ultimate dependence upon a reality, or realities, which control, directly or indirectly, whatever they regard as the essential goods of life. Whatever is regarded as essential to life, therefore, may acquire religious significance.

Fire, for example, acquires such significance in regions of the earth where men in one way or another are dependent upon fire. Wherever men cannot endure the cold winters without fire, there fire is of supreme significance, because it is necessary to life. But man's dependence upon fire becomes an element in his religious life only when he regards particular fires as signs referring to a reality even more important. A particular fire on the hearth of a home, for example, has religious significance only when it is an expression of the "life-sustaining power" of fire. It is this generalization of the life-sustaining character of fire which underlies the worship of

Agni by the Aryans who entered India. The life-sustaining power of fire is, for these Aryans, the nature of Agni, god of fire. As a deity, therefore, Agni is not a particular hearth fire, but that which sustains each and every individual hearth fire, and as such is an ultimate life-sustaining power manifested in every hearth fire.

There would be no religious interpretation without this generalizing capacity of human minds to distinguish between a particular thing essential to life and a reality upon which it is dependent. A religious interpretation of any object of utmost significance in man's life always refers beyond particular instances of it to another reality. The constancy with which all hearth fires, for example, sustain life is something other than the particular fires which glow and then die out.

A particular hearth fire which dies out would never be acknowledged as a reality upon which men are ultimately dependent. The same may be said about millet for the Ainus, grubs for the Australian tribe, and corn for the Navahos. A particular fire for the religious Aryan is a sign of another reality—the life-sustaining power upon which he acknowledges his final dependence. The particular millet which a religious Ainu harvests is likewise a sign of a life-sustaining power expressed through millet, but which is other than all millet. Thus there would be no religion without an ability to distinguish essential factors in human life from an ultimate determinant of their availability for human life.

The way in which food, for example, acquires religious significance may be seen in Aristotle's analysis of the dependence of all life upon food. "Nothing grows," he declares, "except what feeds itself," and "if deprived of food, it must cease to be." Since man cannot live without food, food has indirectly the significance of life itself. "What is fed," Aristotle further says, "is the besouled body."[16] "Essentially related to what has soul in it," the significance of food in man's life is an essential part of the significance of his life. A depreciation of food, therfore, as an unspiritual "concession" to the body is a point of view maintained only by those who do not honestly acknowledge the indispensability of food for human life. The petition in the Lord's prayer for "daily bread," on the other hand, attests the spiritual honesty of Jesus in acknowledging such indispensability.

Dependence upon food is characteristic of all life. But if religion is not to be inclusive of all life, animal as well as human, a distinction must be made between a dependence of life upon food and an acknowledgment of such dependence. All men are dependent upon food. Consequently such dependence is not unique to religious life. What is unique to religious life is the acknowledgment of man's ultimate dependence upon a reality which is not subject to "growth and decay," as is the food which sustains his life. This distinction between the things upon which man immediately depends, and a reality in turn which ultimately controls them, is essential to religious life; and without this distinction, there would be no religious life, no matter how dependent man actually was, and no matter how aware he was of his dependent nature. Man is religious only when he is aware of his dependent nature in relation to an ultimate reality upon which he acknowledges his final dependence.

What men do to acknowledge such dependence is one factor which differentiates human cultures. But what is not a matter of culture is the earnest effort to do all that is believed to be appropriate for acknowledging such dependence. This specifically religious effort includes all that men regard as suitable for acknowledging their dependent status in relation to a reality they revere as ultimately determinative of their lives and all they cherish.

The reference beyond human life to a reality transcendent of it, and transcendent also of the physical context in which men live, is the latitude introduced into human life by religious faith. Religious faith, even on the most primitive level of human life, is an extension of the horizons of life to take a reality into account which is acknowledged to have final control over all that man possesses. Thus insofar as men are religious they become aware of a reality of which the nonreligious are not aware. This awareness is not confined to any particular type of culture. It is a universal aspect of human life, and so includes all that men do to acknowledge their ultimate dependence upon a reality revered as transcendent both of human resources and the physical world.

Chapter Two

RELIGIOUS LIFE

1. *Only realities of utmost importance to individuals have religious significance for them*

If all the realities which, at one time or another, have had religious significance were to be catalogued, the list would include nearly every conceivable thing. In spite of this vast extent, however, all of these realities would have one feature in common. They would all have been of utmost importance to someone.

(a) *The religious significance of food*

Corn, for the Navaho Indians, is a reality of utmost importance, and so it appears as an element in their religious life. One feature of their "pollen prayer" is a ritual in which "a pinch of corn pollen" is taken from a sack in the presence of all who participate. Another feature is the Blessing Chant, in the preparation for which, the family dwelling is consecrated by placing cornmeal "on or above four roof beams in the cardinal directions."[1] Part of this Chant is a "sand painting" ritual, which consists of making "colored designs of cornmeal" on a background of sand.

Corn is so important in the life of the Navahos that it appears in the creation myth accounting for their origin. In this myth, the first Navahos were said to have been made of corn, and they cite their origin from corn as an explanation for their having eaten it ever since. Corn is also of preeminent importance in the life of the Zuñi Indians, and so it assumes an essential place in their religion. In one Zuñi prayer, repeated reference is made to corn, and to the "outstretched hands of water (that) will embrace the corn."[2]

Anyone acquainted with the Old Testament history of the Philistines knows about Dagan, an agricultural deity whose name derives from the term for "corn."[3] Thus the reference to Dagan and his temple in *I Chronicles*[4] links a part of history recorded in the Old Testament with the religions both of primitive peoples and of civilized agricultural peoples. Included in this later category are the ancient Egyptians, for whom Osiris was a vegetation deity of primary importance. He was introduced into Egypt from Western Asia, and was at first regarded by Egyptians as "the spirit of corn." As such he was symbolically represented in tombs by a heap of corn. Since the growth of corn in Egypt depends upon water from the Nile, Osiris in time became identified with the Nile. Hence the religion of the highly civilized Egyptians shares an elemental feature in common with the primitive Navahos and Zuñis. Although there is a vast difference in the attributes of Osiris and a corn-totem for primitive Indians, there is an elemental basis common to both. It is dependence upon a food acknowledged to be derived from a power other than the food itself.

The necessity for food in man's life, whether he be primitive or civilized, accounts for the religious significance of whatever is believed to be ultimately determinative of its availability. The religion of a people includes everything they do to take into account a reality upon which they acknowledge their ultimate dependence for making available to them whatever is of utmost significance in their life. Food is one instance of a reality of such significance.

(b) *The religious significance of rain*

The Zuñi Indians of western New Mexico are extremely tenacious of their ancient religion, and a considerable part of their collective effort is devoted to their cults, among which are cults of water-spirits and of the sun. Water is specifically of religious significance for the Zuñis because it is believed to refer to water-spirits, or kachinas. The "kachina cult" expresses the Zuñi belief "in the existence of a large group of supernatural beings, the kachinas, who live in a lake and are identified with clouds and rain."[5] A Zuñi is respectful to these water spirits because he believes they in turn will be beneficent to him, and one evidence of their beneficence is the rain which makes his corn grow.

The life-sustaining function of rain accounts for the significance of rain in the life of any people dependent upon crops for their food. When this dependence is acknowledged in ways which take into account not only the food, and not only the rain, but a reality transcendent of both, then men are religious in what they do to acknowledge their dependence upon such a reality.

The dependence of human life upon food is not peculiar to primitive people. What is peculiar to them is the narrow margin between life and death due to the limited resources of their food, and due also to their limited means for extending control over the availability of their food. Civilized men are ultimately confronted by the same dependence. Thus the difference between primitive and civilized men in this respect is only a matter of degree. The great civilization of Egypt depended upon its harvests, and this fact was acknowledged in everything that the Egyptians did to revere Osiris, "the great god of fertility," "the god of the fertilizing water."[6] Because the water essential to the Egyptian harvests came from the Nile, the Nile had religious significance for them through its identification with Osiris.

Common to all agricultural people is a dependence upon crops, which involves a dependence upon water. When crops are watered directly by rain, it is rain which has a preeminent significance in their lives. The ancient Hittites, for example, were dependent directly upon rain for their crops, and insofar as they were religious, they revered a "Weather God," "who rules over rain and thunderstorm."[2] It was their acknowledged dependence upon a reality other than rain which made rain of religious significance for them, just as it was for the Egyptians, and for the American Indians. When man's dependence upon rain is acknowledged, and the acknowledgment refers beyond rain to a reality believed to be ultimately determinative of it, then, and then alone, is rain interpreted from a religious point of view. Such a point of view was common not only among the Hittites, but also among the Canaanites, who believed that "the sky and the rains were in the hands of Baal," and who therefore regarded rain-watered land as "land of Baal."

Thunder is associated with rain, and hence it is understandable why Baal should also be regarded as "lord of the thunder." When revered as "lord of the thunder," he was called "the Crasher," or "Rider on the Clouds."[8] These very figures reveal a religious point of view, since they imply an acknowledgment of a power other than the thunder. This reference beyond the thunder to the "lord of the thunder" is a transition from a natural phenomenon to a reality transcendent of it. Without this reference there would be no religious significance of thunder as a natural phenomenon.

This differentiation, which is essential to a religious interpretation, was made by the ancient Chinese. They distinguished between rain and Shang-ti, Lord of Heaven, who is more ultimate than rain. The sacrificial offerings brought by the Emperor and other high officials to the "sun, moon, stars, the clouds, the rain, the wind, and the thunder"[9] are religious acts, since these heavenly bodies and these natural phenomena were regarded as referring beyond themselves to Shang-ti, Lord of Heaven. Sacrificial rites directed to clouds, wind, thunder, and rain would not be religious, no matter how reverent the acts, unless the realities to which they are directed are believed to be ultimate, in the sense that there is believed to be no other reality upon which they are finally dependent.

The sacrificial rites performed on the altar of Earth at the summer solstice are religious acts insofar as the sacrifices were not made to the physical earth, but to the "good genius of the earth" or to "earth kingdom." Whatever the interpretation may be of the reality to which the sacrifices are made, sacrifices are religiously motivated when they express man's attempt to acknowledge his dependence upon an ultimate reality, transcendent of all other realities which are of importance in his life.

This same distinction is made in the popular Hindu interpretation of Brahmaputra, one of the three great rivers of India, upon which millions are dependent for their lives. The water of this river is essential to a vast section of

India, but its indispensability alone does not account for its religious significance. What specifically makes it religiously significant is its interpretation as "Son of Brahma," since this interpretation implies a reference beyond the river to Brahma, the Creator.

Hinduism, as a name for a religion, as well as a social system is derived from the Sanskrit *sindhu*, which means "river." This derivation is instructive, for it illustrates the significance which rivers have always had in the life of India. The most ancient Indian literature is the Vedas, the oldest of which is the Rig-Veda, comprised of a thousand hymns to the gods. Many of these hymns are "references to the rivers of the Indus system."[10]

The relation between food and the water of a river accounts in part for the revered character of the Ganges, the Indus, and the Brahmaputra of India, as well as the Nile of Egypt. The religious significance of these rivers, however, cannot be accounted for merely in terms of a people's dependence upon food, which grows only when watered by a river. Their religious significance rather is a specific consequence of the point of view of a people which refers beyond a river to a reality upon which the river itself is believed to be contingent. A religious point of view is an instance of a mentality which interprets some realities as signs of other realities. For example, Indra, the most prominent deity of the Rig-Veda, was religiously interpreted when revered not as thunder, but as "the wielder of the thunderbolt." The Canaanites' reverence for Baal was a religious experience because Baal was revered not as the thunder, but as "Lord of the thunder."

(c) *The religious significance of heavenly bodies*

Heavenly bodies, especially the sun, are religiously significant for many people, but ordinarily their significance is derivative. It derives from the function which these bodies perform in man's life. The connection between sun and crops is made by every people, primitive as well as civilized. It is for this reason that the sun, as chief of the heavenly bodies for most people, has acquired a pre-eminent place in religions. It heats the earth, and not only gives warmth for the growth of plants, but also determines the seasons for their growth. Although the sun has been worshiped as the ultimate reality by some ancient peoples, there is also evidence that other ancient peoples made a distinction between the physical sun and a sun god. Amen-Ra, sun-god for the early Egyptians, for example, was conceived as "the lord of all being," and when so interpreted, it is understandable why the Nile itself should be regarded as a gift of Amen-Ra.

The Sumerians worshiped the sun-god Shemash, whose importance in ancient civilizations is indicated by the spread of his significance among all the eastern Semites. His influence even in Israel is revealed by the references in the Old Testament to places such as Beth-Shemesh, "House of the Sun," and En Shemesh, "Spring of the Sun."[11]

The Aryans who entered India worshiped the solar deity Mitra, and the Aryans who entered the Iranian plateau worshiped the solar deity Mithra. Hence Mitra of the Vedas and Mithra of the Avesta are the same. Their identity in two great bodies of religious literature, the Vedas of Hinduism and the Avesta of Zoroastrianism, testifies to the pre-eminent importance of the sun in two great cultures derived from Indo-European sources. A reference to Mithra in the Avesta as "the Lord of wide pastures" is an acknowledgment by an agricultural people of an ultimate dependence for pasturage upon a reality transcendent of the earth. Mithra was the supreme object of worship for early Persians, and there is some basis to believe that as god of light he was not always identified with the physical sun, but was also revered as more ultimate than the sun. It is as god of light that Mithra became the *deus Sol invictus Mithra* worshiped in the Roman empire in the early centuries of the Christian era.

(d) *The religious interpretation of the fertility of fields*

The agricultural basis of Roman civilization accounts for the innumerable deities of the fields, one of which assumed prominence over all the others. This was Mars, who originally was not a war god, but was rather a protector of the fields. His protective function may thus account for the shift which later occurred when he became protector of the Empire, and so god of war. The same role which Mars fulfilled in the religious life of the early agricultural people of Rome was fulfilled for the early Greeks by Demeter. As patroness of agriculture, her significance for an agricultural people is disclosed in the very calendar of her festivals, the chief of which occurred in the planting season. She was identified with fertility—not only the fertility of the fields, but also of human life. As a consequence of this extension of her significance, she was worshiped throughout Greece as the Great Goddess. Acknowledged to be other than the fertility of fields, cattle, and people, she was revered as the ultimate determiner of all fertility.

This distinction, however, is not a feature peculiar to later Greek civilization. It was also made by the prehistoric Greeks who regarded particular trees as sacred because embodiments of a "divinity of vegetation." Although this distinction occurred in the prehistoric culture of Greece, it was not always a feature of the religious life either of the prehistoric Greeks or of the later Greeks. Primitive mentality is always at hand, and this mentality does not always make clear distinctions. It is for this reason that trees themselves were worshiped at the same time that trees were regarded as embodiments of a divinity other than the trees. At the same time that some of the Minoan-Mycenaean people worshiped the divinity of vegetation embodied in a tree, others worshiped the tree itself. Hence "palms, cypress, pines, fig trees—and even boughs were worshiped."[12]

Individuals without a capacity to regard one reality as a sign of another reality are incapable of revering a tree as an embodiment of a reality other than the tree itself. For them, the tree itself is an object of reverence. It is only when individuals are capable of regarding one reality as a sign of another reality that physical objects can be revered, and yet not worshiped.

The tree cult of the prehistoric Greeks is an acknowledgment of man's ultimate dependence upon some reality responsible for the fertility of the soil, and this acknowledgment expresses a religious point of view. For one type of mentality, a tree itself is revered. For another mentality, a tree may be regarded as a sign, referring to a reality upon which its growth, as well as the growth of all trees and all vegetation, is ultimately dependent. Thus two fundamentally different interpretations of an object may occur within the same culture.

Individuals of every possible gradation of intelligence and culture may be religious provided they acknowledge that they are confronted by a reality upon which they are ultimately dependent. But the interpretation of this reality is always conditioned by the capacities of individuals. People without a capacity to understand their dependence upon a reality other than trees sometimes revere trees as if no other reality more significant could be comprehended. It is this inability to understand the nature of an ultimate reality upon which human life actually is dependent that accounts for some primitive people's worship of trees. Individuals who do not understand the nature of an ultimate reality may, however, be regarded as religious insofar as they do all that they can within the limits of their capacities to acknowledge their dependence upon what they believe to be supremely significant for their life.

This interpretation of religions as a type of human life, therefore, ignores culture as an essential determinant of religious life. But it does acknowledge the effect of culture upon religious life. An individual may be religious even though he worships a tree, provided he cannot comprehend that there is a reality more significant in his life than the tree he reveres. When one does all that he can to give his utmost respect to any reality upon which he acknowledges his ultimate dependence, he has done all that he can in his religious life. What one is capable of doing sets limits to what he does, and although what one does may be less than he is capable of doing, no one can do more than he has the capacities to do. This is stressing the same fact which is acknowledged in the New Testament parable of the talents. The point of view with which religions are interpreted in this study is, therefore, nothing other than an application of this parable to the religious life of mankind.

(e) *The religious acknowledgment of a spirit of fertility*

Man's dependence upon the soil, both for his life and for the life of his family, is acknowledged when he reveres a reality which he believes is ultimately responsible for the fertility of fields. The ways in which men acknowledge such dependence differ as do the cultures of mankind. In spite of such cultural differences, the religious motive, wherever it is expressed, has a common character. It is the earnest attempt of men to do what they believe is appropriate for taking into account their dependence upon a reality other than their own resources.

All people whose lives depend upon the productivity of the soil are confronted with the stern fact that although man does all he can, still what he can do is not enough to insure the growth of his crops. When this much reflection has occurred in human life, there is a basis for a religious interpretation of man's relation to another reality upon which he is ultimately dependent, and before this much reflection takes place there can be no specifically religious effort. Religious efforts express men's earnest desires to take into account all that they revere as ultimately significant in determining all that they value. One expression of such religious effort is the creation of religiously significant symbols. But it must be acknowledged that men no more create their dependence upon the earth than they create the productivity of the earth. They merely create the symbols with which they acknowledge their dependence.

One of these symbols is a mother-goddess, or the Earth Mother. This symbol occurs in one form or another throughout the world, but in whatever form it occurs, it is an expression of man's effort to designate a life-sustaining power which is manifested in every thing upon which his life ultimately depends. When this power is symbolized, the most natural symbol to be selected is a mother from whom one receives his own life. The symbol of the earth mother is a means for designating an ultimate reality controlling the fertility of the soil, of the crops, of cattle, and of human life.

This symbol is man's acknowledgment of a reality other than the physical earth that undergoes the fluctuation of drought and storm which ruins his crops and so impairs his life. When man believes that there is a reality other than the earth upon which the earth depends for its fruitfulness, he interprets both the earth and a reality other than the earth from a religious point of view, and he does what seems to him to be appropriate for acknowledging his ultimate dependence upon this transcendent reality.

Neolithic figurines of clay, representing a mother-goddess, have been found in great numbers in Iran. This type of symbol used in Iran thousands of years B.C. is an instance of the same symbolic phenomenon which occurred in ancient Indus civilizations. Having cultural roots in common with the Aryans of the Indus valley, the Iranians used symbols similar to those of their ancestors in the Indus valley, and one characteristic of the Indus civilization was the worship of a mother-goddess, or the Earth Mother.

All ancient civilizations which emerged in the Mediterranean region and in Asia Minor depend directly upon the productivity of the soil, and therefore the religions of these civilizations took account of the pre-eminent significance of the fertility of the soil.

The chief goddess of the Babylonian pantheon was Ishtar, who as Earth Mother personified the reproductive forces of nature. The Phoenician symbol for the same forces was Astarte. The Ashtoreth mentioned in the Old Testament is but another name for this reality, and Isis of the Egyptians, Aphrodite of the Greeks, Venus of the Romans are all designations of this same reality of utmost significance in human life. Diana of Ephesus was another symbolic form of the Great Mother revered by the Ancients. Thus it is understandable why the Ephesians should not readily acquiesce to the preaching of St. Paul, but should continue to call out "for the space of two hours," "Great is Diana."

(f) *The religious significance of the family*

Just as the fertility of the soil is an indispensable condition for man's life, so is human fertility a condition both for his individual and his corporate life. Irrespective of culture, therefore, human fertility is of utmost significance, and for this reason is included among men's religious concerns. The importance of a family, not only for an individual's survival and well-being, but also for the very possibility of corporate life, is basic to the complex system of obligations which have developed in the course of centuries in the so-called Chinese "Ancestor worship." So important is an individual's fulfillment of his obligations to his family, that an appreciable aspect of his life consists in what he does to discharge these responsibilities. The family, including even remote ancestors, has consequently acquired a significance in the life of many Chinese which involves features characteristic of religious life.

But if religion is not to be a synonym for morality, or a type of morality, moral motivation must be differentiated from religious motivation. A moral motivation is an effort to do all one can with his own resources for the enhancement of human life, his own or that of others. A religious motivation, on the other hand, is man's effort to do all that he believes is worthy of him in his relation to a reality he reveres as the ultimate determiner of all that he cherishes in his life. Insofar as this may be said of the Chinese who revere their ancestors, the ancestor worship of China may be regarded as one type of religious life. But when Chinese ancestor worship is included in the category of religion, it presupposes a distinction between the ancestor who died, and that part of the ancestor which continues to affect an individual's life. This distinction is made by the Chinese, since underlying even the most devout Chinese ancestor worship is a primitive animistic point of view, according to which the spirit of a person lives on after death. When this distinction between two orders of reality is made, the offerings given to the departed are adjustments to realities believed to be ultimately determinative of an individual's life. It is on this ground that Chinese, as well as Hindu, feasts to ancestors are motivated by the religious acknowledgment of man's dependence for his welfare upon realities transcendent of his life and of the physical world. The dualistic distinction between an individual who lives in the physical world and the soul of an individual which persists after death is, therefore, essential for classifying ancestor rites as "worship." To be classified as "worship," the rites must not only refer to a spirit which has no spatial location, but the spirit must be regarded as ultimately determinative of the welfare of those who do have such a location.

2. *Religious life is a reference beyond human life and human resources*

A reference to a reality transcendent of human life is essential to religious life. Such an orientation of human life to a reality other than human life is a feature of religion which is irrespective of culture. But what man does in this reference beyond his life is conditioned by his culture. Few people would have the language ability to declare as Tersteegen, "My spirit to that source must turn for which it hath been made to live," but every religious person, regardless of his culture, shares with this spiritually gifted mystic the earnest endeavor to orient his life, as reverently as he is able, to a reality upon which he acknowledges his ultimate dependence.

(a) *Religious life is an attempt to understand the nature of a reality transcendent of human life*

Religious life is a turning from man's resources and the physical world, from which he directly derives his resources, to a reality he regards as ultimately determinative of their availability. This reference beyond human life and the physical world to a reality man acknowledges to be ultimately determinative of all he values is an elemental feature of his religious life. Every such reference is conditioned by his abilities, but his attempt to take into account a reality transcendent of his life, for its significance in his life, is not an expression either of his culture or of his abilities.

Religious life is an acknowledgment that there is a supremely significant reality which man must acknowledge if he is to understand all that he ought to do in his life. Underlying all religious life, therefore, is an earnest effort to understand the nature of the total context in which man lives, and the total environment to which he must make his adjustment. The fact that the ritual of primitive people is often so bewildering to men of a more developed culture ought not to prevent an appreciative understanding of the underlying motive for such behavior. The ritual of primitive men is their attempt, within the limits of their abilities, to take into account their relation to a reality other than their own lives, and other than their own resources, because it is believed to be a final determinant of their lives and their resources. What people of a primitive culture do to acknowledge their dependence, and what they do to relate themselves to a reality upon which they acknowledge their final dependence, is an expression both of what they know and of what they do not know. This twofold conditioning of interpretation is as characteristic of the most advanced of sciences and philosophies in modern civilizations as it is of the crudest rites in the most primitive of cultures. What men earnestly do expresses what they believe is appropriate. Their belief about what is appropriate is conditioned by their opportunities to acquire an informed understanding of the nature of the context in which they live. But irrespective of such knowledge, the motive to do earnestly all that men believe is appropriate in their various relationships is not a peculiarity of culture. This motive is a feature of human life.

Wherever men live, they try to do what they believe to be appropriate for working out their relations to what they regard as essential to their lives. Just as the implements which primitive peoples use have little similarity to the implements used in technically advanced societies, so do many rituals of primitive communities have little superficial similarity to the ceremonial practices of civilized cultures. But underlying the most primitive and the most civilized is the same fundamental motive. It is to do everything that men can do with the facilities they have to take into account all they believe to be essential for the achievement of what they most cherish.

What men with such motivation do is conditioned by their intelligence. But the motive to do all that they are able to do is not a matter of their intelligence. For example, primitive men, just as civilized men, try to account for reflections of objects. The science of optics, however, is not one of the achievements either of primitive culture or of early civilizations, and for this reason the explanations proposed for such phenomena, both by primitive men and by men of early civilizations, are not scientifically informed. The early Hittites interpreted the reflection of the sun on water as a second sun, and so they believed there were two suns, and two sun-gods—the sun-god in the heavens, and the sun-god in the water.

Whether one classifies this interpretation in Hittite civilization as religion, or as science, makes no basic difference. The fact is that religion and science both express what men believe. What they believe in their science can't help but reflect, in some way, in what they do in their religious life. When men understand little of the nature of the physical world, their religious life reveals the limits of their general knowledge. But this fact does not imply that religious life is a function of intelligence or culture. Intelligence and culture make a difference in what men do to acknowledge their relation to a reality they revere as more ultimate than human life, and more ultimate than the physical world in which they live. Primitive Australian aborigines, for example, do not even understand so elementary a phenomenon as the role of a father in the birth of a child. For them, a father's role is "providing the mother with food."[13] When so elementary an aspect of life is not understood, it is not surprising that these primitive people should reveal equally limited knowledge in their religious life. Conditioned though their religious life may be by their intelligence, their motive to use whatever intelligence they have to acknowledge their dependence upon a reality more ultimate than their life and the physical world is not culturally determined.

Primitive men, and people living in civilized cultures who have the intellectual equipment of primitives, do not understand even the most elementary aspects of their lives. Such ignorance, therefore, is not to be chronologically classified. It has nothing essentially to do with an historical age. It is rather an expression of the limits of human understanding in any age. Even today under the very shadow of the learned institutions in India, there are millions of people with the limited knowledge of primitive men. For this reason, they do what primitive men do. This fact applies to their religious life, just as it applies to every other aspect of their life. Women in modern India still revere the pipal tree, which is a species of fig tree allied to the banyan, because they associate its milky white sap with human fertility. Wanting children, Indian women with the mentality of primitives make offerings to the pipal tree in the hope that they may have children. The belief that there is a connection between the sap of a tree and the birth of a child is not peculiar to the religion of this people. It is rather an expression of their limited understanding of the nature of birth, and of the conditions for birth. There is, therefore, no more basis for identifying this instance of ignorance with religion than there is for identifying it with their philosophy or their science. If they were to formulate a philosophy of life, or a science of the nature of birth, they would reveal the same amount of ignorance in these as they do in their religion.

A basis, however, for classifying their sacrificial offering to the pipal tree as a religious act is its underlying motive. These women who want children do all they believe can be done to bring about their motherhood. Hence it is not the sacrificial character of their offering to the pipal tree which constitutes the basis for its classification as religious, but rather the motive which impels the sacrifice. The tree is revered because it is believed to be ultimately determinative of a good of utmost importance in their lives.

What people do not understand, they nevertheless interpret as best they can. The "best they can" is always an expression of their cultural opportunities, and hence religion, just as science, bears the indelible marks of culture.

(b) *What men do not understand they regard as mysterious*

People who do not understand the complex phenomenon of birth, nevertheless do in their ignorance what seems to them to be suitable for handling this aspect of human life. Included in what they believe is suitable are all the prohibitions and taboos which have become associated with birth and with parenthood. The bathing ceremonials of the Jains of India, for example, are attempts to cope with the bewildering phenomena associated with birth and with parenthood. Even the father is required to undergo ceremonial bathing after the birth of a child before he may again enter into his full social activities. Incredibly ignorant as this may appear to people with a knowledge of modern biology, the bathing rite is understandable on the principle of association. Bathing is assumed to remove "uncleanness" associated with birth, and ceremonial "uncleanness" is an expression of what men do not understand. What is not understood is mysterious, and what is mysterious is feared. Thus as features of human life, ignorance and fear have nothing essentially to do with particular cultures.

Any means may be used by men in their endeavor to control occasions provocative of fear and of the sense of mystery associated with what is feared. Hence, neither fear nor the sense of mystery is peculiar to religion. The sense of mystery is a function of ignorance, and the less men know of the nature of their life and the nature of the world in which they live, the greater is the number of the things they fear, and the greater also is the number of things they regard as mysterious.

Notwithstanding the advantages of the most enlightened civilized life, there is always much that is not known. A basis, however, for the differentiation of primitive and civilized life is what is known, rather than what is not known. If ignorance were to be the basis for a classification of cultures, all cultures would justifiably be classified in one category. But when knowledge makes an appreciable difference in the quality of life, and in what men do, knowledge is of great significance, and so rightly becomes a basis for a fundamental distinction between cultures. Yet fundamental as knowledge is in the distinction of primitive culture from civilized culture, it does not constitute an essential feature of a universal type of human life, such as religion.

What primitive men do not understand they regard as mysterious, and so they project a feature of their lives onto a reality other than themselves. This projection, however, in one form or another, is common to all human life, and so is no more peculiar to primitive life than it is to some aspects of civilized life, and it is no more peculiar to the religious aspect of life than it is to other aspects of human life. Hence it is indefensible to regard projection as a unique feature of religious life, or even as essential to it.

When man acknowledges his dependence upon a reality upon which he actually is dependent, such as the fertility of the soil, or any number of other factors essential to his life, he does not project a feature of his life upon a reality external to his life. When he understands that he is dependent upon the fertility of the soil, for example, he understands the actual status of his life as dependent. When, however, he personifies the fertility of the soil as a goddess, and conceives the features of the goddess in his own image, then he does project. But this projection is a feature of his symbolism. It is not essential to religious life, even though it may be included in religious life. A religious life is possible which includes neither pictorial symbolism nor projection. When man acknowledges with reverence that he is ultimately dependent upon a reality other than his resources, and other than the physical world itself, he interprets his life and the world religiously. In this interpretation he need not introduce any symbols which express features of his own nature. For this reason it is indefensible to regard projection as essential to religion. It is not essential to religion any more than it is essential to any other aspect of human life in which man endeavors to interpret the nature of the total context in which he lives.

One aspect of the context in which man lives is interpreted in his science. Another aspect is interpreted in his religious life, and his religious interpretation may be as free as his science from a projection of his nature onto a reality transcendent of himself. A science of the moon no more rests upon an interpretation of a "man in the moon" than does religion rest upon a reverence for a divine reality made in man's image.

Some realities which men fear are not created in their imaginations, and some realities which they revere are not fabrications of their fancies. There are many aspects of the physical context in which men struggle for their lives which actually threaten their lives, and which must be taken into account if they are to live. Man's concern, therefore, to take into account all he believes to be directly or indirectly significant for his well-being is not an expression of mental abnormality. The identification of all religious life with mental abnormality is, therefore, a point of view which is too absurd to state even for the purpose of refuting. The anxiety which a primitive individual experiences when he sees the progressive destruction of his crops by drought is no more pathological than is his earnest effort to do what he believes is appropriate to acknowledge his relation to a reality which he believes is ultimately determinative of the weather, of his crops, and so of his life. The same concern occurs today when people stand helpless before a drought which cancels not only their hard work, but also puts their well-being and the welfare of their families into jeopardy. Confronted by such a crisis, primitive and civilized men alike are brought face to face, not with a projection, but with a reality other than themselves.

Religion includes all that men do to acknowledge their ultimate dependence upon a reality which they regard as dependable enough to warrant their most earnest efforts to relate themselves to it for its contribution to their lives. What men do to relate themselves to such a reality includes all of the prohibitions which delimit the latitude of human behavior in relation to a reality revered as other than human life and other than human possessions. Among such prohibitions are the taboos of primitive life, which are the serious attempts of primitive men to define the limits that they must respect in their relations to the reality whose supreme importance in their lives they cannot ignore.

Birth and parenthood are events in human life of utmost importance, and it is for this reason that innumerable taboos have arisen in primitive life to take their significance into account. The intended function of a taboo in primitive life should not be analyzed as "the elimination of fear." The intended function of a taboo is not to control an experience, but to safeguard a possession of utmost significance in human life.

(c) *A sense of the mysterious is not an essential feature of religious experience*

Occurrences which individuals do not understand often are regarded as mysterious. Although an analysis of ignorance as a factor accounting for a classification of some events as mysterious is psychologically defensible, it is not defensible to identify the sense of mystery with the essential nature of religious experience. Such an identification is purely arbitrary. This identification, however, is made by those who maintain that events which are not understandable are placed by religious people in the "category of the mysterious," which is a category essential to religious life. This identification of the sense of mystery with religious experience is a definition of religion in terms of what is not understood, and as such it is arbitrary. What is arbitrary is not the analysis of the sense of mystery as a consequence of ignorance. It is rather the identification of the sense of mystery with the essence of religion. This identification is not only arbitrary; it is a distortion of the actual data traditionally classified as religiously significant.

When the sense of mystery is regarded as essential to religious life, all religious behavior is interpreted as basically motivated by ignorance. This becomes clear in an analysis of the religious significance of food, when it is maintained that the "most striking feature" in "the food-quest" is "the sense of mystery." That this analysis is an accommodation to the identification of mystery with religion is almost too obvious to mention. The purely arbitrary aspect of this analysis becomes apparent, for example, in an explanation of the "great religious significance" of the Nile as due to its mysterious origin: "a perpetual mystery also its inundation."[14] That the origin of the Nile and its inundations were not understood by the ancient Egyptians need not be questioned. What may be questioned, however, is the warrant for selecting the fact of ignorance of the origin of the Nile and of its inundations as the basis for its religious significance.

An alternative analysis of the religious significance of the Nile is the dependence of the Egyptians upon it for their life. The fact of their dependence they understood, even though they did not understand the phenomenon of its periodic inundations. They understood very clearly that their crops could not grow without the Nile, and they in turn could not live without its water. The life-sustaining character of the Nile was one thing the Egyptians did understand, and in understanding their dependence upon the Nile, they treated it as a reality of supreme importance in their lives. They were clearly aware that their crops disappeared with its recession and returned when its waters returned. Thus they knew that they depended upon the constancy of the return of the waters of the Nile for their crops, and so for their life. Such constancy they could not regard as a feature of the water of the Nile. Referring beyond the Nile to a reality in terms of which they accounted for the periodic recurrence of its waters, which they could predict, and which they could hopefully anticipate, they interpreted the ordered phenomenon of the Nile as Heraclitus, the Greek philosopher, interpreted the ordered character of the physical world. Heraclitus interpreted the order which men observe in the physical world in terms of the Logos. Although the Logos is not observed as a feature of the physical world, it was, nevertheless, acknowledged by Heraclitus as an ultimate explanatory factor for the order which is observed in the physical world. Why should anyone, therefore, who does not regard the metaphysic of Heraclitus as an expression of ignorance arbitrarily classify the religious life of the ancient Egyptians as an instance of their ignorance? The reference of the Egyptians beyond the Nile to a reality more ultimate than it is a metaphysic which underlies its religious significance for them. To analyze its religious significance entirely as a consequence of what they did not understand is to press historical data into an arbitrary category.

When the sense of mystery is selected as the essential nature of religious life, it follows that all religious beliefs are interpreted in terms of what man does not understand. Rather than interpreting religious adjustment as man's attempt to take into account a reality transcendent of his experience, his religious adjustment is interpreted as a response to experience, motivated by ignorance. Thus the significance of the Nile in the religious life of the Egyptians is, according to this point of view, an expression of their failure to understand the nature of the Nile. What, however, is of primary significance in their relation to the Nile is not its mystery, but their dependence upon it for its indispensability in their life.

Clearly understanding that they could not live without its life-sustaining waters, the Egyptians were equally clear about their dependence upon whatever ultimately determined the phenomena associated with the Nile. Hence their belief that the Nile is a gift of Amen Ra, the sun-god. This is not an analysis of experience. It is rather an interpretation of the Nile in relation to a reality beyond it. It is, therefore, a distortion of Egyptian history to regard the religious significance of the Nile as an instance exclusively of the sense of mystery. Their actual dependence upon the Nile accounts for its pre-eminent place in their culture, and accounts specifically for its significance in their religious life. Its religious significance is a consequence of their clear understanding that they depended upon the Nile for their livelihood, and therefore they were ultimately dependent upon a reality determinative of its predictable order.

This reference beyond the Nile to an ultimate reality is a metaphysic which underlies the religious significance of the Nile in the life of the Egyptians. Hence its religious significance cannot be accounted for by a psychological analysis of the sense of mystery, which derives from an inability to understand. "The simplest type of religion" does not arise "from that basic tendency to ascribe power to that which man finds mysterious." Confronted by realities other than himself, before which he is aware of his insufficiency and his helplessness, man becomes religious when he acknowledges his final dependence upon a reality he trusts as ultimately dependable, and so able to contribute to his life what no other reality can. The "simplest type of religion," therefore, involves a reference beyond man's life, just as every type of religion does. There is no religion, and no religious life, without man's acknowledgment of his final dependence upon an ultimate reality which he trusts as dependable for its supplementation of his dependent life.

"The sense of mystery in things which attract his attention but which he cannot understand" is not the "taproot of all religion." It is only a feature which occurs in some religious life, and it occurs when man is more impressed with what he does not understand than he is with what he understands. There are limits to what is understood in all cultures, and for this reason, ignorance is no more peculiar to religious life than it is to any other aspect of human life. Insofar as any reality which is not understood is mysterious to man, the sense of mystery is a function of his ignorance. But man's acknowledgment of his dependence upon realities whose indispensability in his life he cannot ignore is not an expression of his ignorance.

Man indicates his intelligence insofar as he takes into account realities with which he is confronted in making his adjustments, and his adjustments are motivated by real information when he takes realities into account with which he actually is confronted. "That sense of the mysterious which comes to primitive man in the face of the multitudes of things he cannot understand" is, therefore, not unique to his religious life. To identify it with religious life is arbitrary, and follows from the arbitrary definition of religion as man's response to what he regards as mysterious.

Any point of view, of course, may be taken as the clue with which to analyze anything, provided one is able to disregard sufficient data to make the procedure cogent. Thus it is possible to interpret every aspect of human life which is religiously significant in terms of any point of view. One such arbitrary point of view is that "the event that passes explanation" is religiously significant because it is not understood, and therefore is mysterious to the individual who does not understand it.

It may be a "fact which Anthropology and Comparative Religion establish beyond a doubt that wherever and in whatever age man is found, he has a tendency to believe in an Unseen Power in whatsoever is mysterious to him." But it is not a "fact" of the same empirical character that the "tendency to believe in an Unseen Power" is to be accounted for in terms of its mysterious nature. This is an interpretation of observable behavior, and it is not purely "factual." It is a point of view with which observable data are interpreted. In this case, it is a point of view which distorts the features of observable data to accommodate them to a bias. The bias is that "the most significant element for the history of religion is the 'numinous' character . . . great in proportion to its mystery, surrounded therefore with awe, with an *aura* of the sacred."[15]

One familiar with Rudolph Otto's book *The Idea of the Holy*, is immediately aware of the influence of Otto in the foregoing analysis of religion as man's response to his sense of mystery. An identification of the mysterious with religion, however, is not unique to Professor Otto. What is unique to him is the bias that "the numinous consciousness" is the "most noteworthy phenomenon in the whole history of religion." Otto is also not the only one to maintain that the "feeling of the numinous" cannot be analyzed in terms of concepts, since any feeling which is distinguishable from other feelings has features peculiar to itself. The uniqueness of the numinous feeling stressed by Professor Otto is psychologically sound, but what is not equally sound is his premise that this "feeling of the numinous" is "the basic factor and the basic impulse underlying the entire process of religious evolution." That it is a factor in some religious experience need not be doubted. When, however, it is maintained that it is "the basic impulse" in the history of religion, it implies that religious life is essentially a response to man's own feeling. Religious life is man's response, but his religious response is his adjustment to a reality other than his life, whose pre-eminent significance in his life he acknowledges. Such acknowledgment is motivated by his awareness that his life is dependent, and yet, in his dependent status he believes there is a dependable reality to which he may turn. The "basic" religious motive is man's endeavor to relate himself to a reality he esteems as being more dependable than the physical world with its many fluctuations, and more worthy of his trust than his own possessions.

Professor Otto is justified in stressing the unique nature of religious life, but he is not equally justified in identifying religious life with "the feeling of the numinous" as its unique feature. He maintains that "the feeling of the numinous . . . is qualitatively *sui generis*." This, however, may be said equally well of any experience which is distinguishable from all other experiences. The significant feature about religious experience is not that it is unique in its "non-rational" features. What is religiously significant about its uniqueness is its reference beyond human life to a reality upon which the very goods most esteemed in life are acknowledged to be ultimately dependent.

Religious life, however, is not merely a conceptual acknowledgment of a reality transcendent of human life. It is rather the earnest attempt of men to do all they believe is worthy of themselves in their relation to this reality upon which they acknowledge their final dependence. This analysis of religious life and of its basic motivation rests upon a point of view which is incompatible with the point of view of Professor Otto, according to whom the numinous is a "state of mind" or a "mental state," which is "absolutely primary." According to the point of view of this essay, it is not primary, but secondary, and as such it is not essential to religious life.

What is essential to religious life is the clear realization that man is finally dependent upon a reality which is not dependent upon any other reality. Hence it is revered by man as ultimate, and religious life includes all that man does to acknowledge his confrontation by such a reality, which he reveres as the final determinant of all that he possesses, or desires to possess.

Aware of his dependent nature, and believing that transcendent of his life and of every other dependent thing there is a reality which depends upon nothing for its nature, man refers beyond his life, to it, for its ultimate determination of his life. Religious life, therefore, cannot be accounted for entirely in terms of experience. Unique though the numinous experience may be in human life, it is not the unique feature of religious life, and, therefore, it is not the factor in terms of which religion as a type of human life may be interpreted. It consequently is not enough to say that "the feeling of one's own abasement, of being but 'dust and ashes' . . . forms the numinous raw material for the feeling of religious humility." Man feels such abasement only when he is aware that he is dependent, and that in spite of his intelligence, and all of his possessions, he is ultimately confronted by the limits of his sufficiency. Keenly aware of his inability to control ultimately what he most cherishes, and clearly aware of his incapacity finally even to retain what he possesses, he acknowledges his status as essentially of "dust and ashes."

But this depreciation of his sufficiency is not uniquely religious. Although a profound religious experience would not be possible without some such awareness of man's confrontation by the limits of his sufficiency, such an awareness is not itself religious experience. It is only one element in religious experience. An individual is religious only when he acknowledges his final dependence upon an ultimate reality, in relation to which he is motivated to do all that he believes it is worthy of him to do to revere it for its supreme significance. For some Egyptians, this was "raising the hand to Ishtar." For some prehistoric Greeks, it was "raising of the hands" to the goddess of the Acropolis of Mycenae. For the Psalmist, it was reverently acknowledging that "The Heavens declare Thy glory."

Professor Otto himself offers such an analysis of religious life, but he does so in spite of the basic premise of his study, and therefore does so only incidentally. When he forgets the strictures of the initial premise with which he proposed to interpret religious life, he maintains that "creature-feeling . . . is the emotion of a creature, abased and overwhelmed by its own nothingness in contrast to that which is supreme above all creatures." This analysis, however, is not consistent with his attempt to give a description of the numinous as a thoroughly non-rational experience. It is rather an analysis of the occasion for "creature-feeling" as religious experience. And it is religious because it is a reference beyond man's life to a reality before which his sufficiency is ultimately nothing more than "dust and ashes."

The reference beyond man's life, which is maintained in this essay to be an essential feature of a specifically religious creature-feeling, is also emphasized by Professor Otto, when he declares that the creature-feeling "has immediate and primary reference to an object outside the self." When he maintains that "this 'feeling of reality,' the feeling of a 'numinous' *object* objectively given must be posited as a primary immediate datum of consciousness,"[16] he likewise maintains as essential to religious life the feature which has been stressed throughout this essay. But his analysis of the "numinous" is not consistent, and its inconsistency is an expression of the ambiguity of the term "numinous." He speaks of "numinous" both as "a feeling" which is unique to human life, and also as a feature of a reality in relation to which man has this feeling.

There is, however, no ambiguity in the use of this term when he specifically analyzed the faith of Islam as an acknowledgment of Allah as "mere 'numen.'" There is also no ambiguity in his specific analysis of the experiences of Peter and Isaiah when they encountered "the numinous reality . . . as a present fact of consciousness." But just as soon as the phrase "fact of consciousness" enters into his analysis, the ambiguity is introduced. It is introduced because, as a Neo-Kantian philosopher, Otto interprets "fact of consciousness" as experience. Yet, the Kantian theory of knowledge which Professor Otto accepts as a philosophical premise is not adequate for analyzing religious experience as a faith in a reality transcendent of human experience, which man can know as the ultimate determiner of all that he cherishes in his life. The basic religious motive to revere a reality transcendent of human life, whose significance in man's life is supreme above other reality, implies a claim to knowledge which is incompatible with Kant's theory, which repudiates the possibility for knowing any reality transcendent of human experience. Yet, Professor Otto assumes the defensibility of Kant's theory as a philosophical analysis of the nature of human knowledge, and so when consistent with the Kantian point of view, he analyzes religious experience as man's response to the sense of the numinous, which is a feature of man's experience.

3. *Religious life is an acknowledged dependence upon a reality regarded as ultimate*

The religious motive for turning to a reality transcendent of human life is that it is believed to be able to contribute to man's life what is of utmost importance to him. What man most desires determines, consequently, the particular realities which have religious significance in his life. But it is the acknowledged indispensability of a reality transcendent of human life which accounts for the turning of religious life beyond itself. What man desires, but does not possess by virtue of his own abilities and his own resources, motivates him to seek beyond his life, and its resources, for the fulfillment of his desires. One such good which is sought in religious life is salvation. In this general category is included all the specific goods which man most cherishes, for the attainment of which he turns beyond himself and his resources to a reality he trusts for its ultimate dependability. The ultimate dependability of the reality to which a religious individual turns is the primary feature of every religious interpretation. Hence a quest for salvation is religiously significant only when motivated by the conviction that it can be attained solely in relation to an ultimate reality, capable of contributing to man's life what no other reality is capable of contributing.

Even Buddhism in its original form may be interpreted as primarily a quest for salvation. A frequently quoted saying attributed to the founder of Buddhism is that just as the ocean is "permeated by only one savor, the savor of salt," so are his teachings "permeated by only one savor, the savor of salvation." The salvation which the disciples of Buddha seek is a release from a type of life which cannot be satisfied by goods which continually refer beyond themselves. From the fact that every good which man desires and acquires reinforces desire rather than satisfies it, Buddha concluded that desire is the root of evil, and maintained that the most cherished life would be freedom from desire. Such freedom, for the Buddha and his disciples, is salvation, or Nirvana.

The Buddhist quest for salvation is a religious phenomenon, and not merely a moral one, since the attainment of Nirvana depends upon acquiring a knowledge of the eternal Dharma, or eternal Law of Life. If Nirvana could be achieved by any technique peculiar to an individual, there would be nothing uniquely religious about it. Nirvana is a goal of religious life because in seeking it, a devout Buddhist refers beyond all human resources and all contingent things to an ultimate reality. This ultimate reality is the Dharma, which, when known, is believed to enable man to attain a type of life he cannot attain by any other means. Essential, therefore, to Buddhism as a religion, rather than as a moral philosophy, is the reference of human life to an ultimate reality transcendent of human resources which is esteemed for its indispensable contribution to human life.

A disciple of Buddha turns to the Dharma that he may know it, and with this knowledge may be dependably directed in his life. This is the enlightened life, and is the only type of life which he supremely desires. It is a life which is not spent in pursuit of goods that do not satisfy, even though they are possessed. It is freedom from such a search, and this freedom is salvation. Sariputta, foremost among the disciples of Gautama, declared, "Nirvana is salvation, Nirvana is salvation."[17]

A clear understanding that every desired good which strengthens desire, but does not satisfy the self even when the desire is temporarily fulfilled, is basic to the enlightenment of a Hinayana Buddhist. This fact, which is not a peculiarity of some individual's lives, but is a universal feature of human life, is a Law of Life. A "knowledge of the perishability of all the fetters of existence" is thus regarded by a Buddhist as an understanding both of the nature of life, and also of a universal law that the nature of life is such that it cannot find its fulfillment in goods which constantly refer beyond themselves. Only the individual who clearly understands the inability of life to be satisfied by goods which reinforce desire without fulfilling it, is, according to the Buddha and his disciples, enlightened. Only the enlightened find salvation from ignorance, with its many delusions. Hence essential to the achievement of Nirvana is "the extinction of desire, . . . the extinction of delusion."

This salvation, which is the goal of a Hinayana Buddhist, is an achievement dependent upon a knowledge of the eternal Dharma, or Law of Life. Without this acknowledged dependence upon an eternal reality for its contribution of a completely dependable good to human life, there would be nothing peculiarly religious in the quest for salvation interpreted as Nirvana. If an "extinguishing of the thirst for life in the world of the senses" could be achieved without any acknowledged dependence upon an eternal law, whose contribution to life is the enlightenment of life, the attainment of Nirvana would be purely a moral phenomenon. But the attainment of Nirvana for a Buddhist is an objective of religious life, because its attainment is believed to depend upon turning to an ultimate reality which is a supremely dependable authority for human life.

The basis on which original Taoism may likewise be classified as a religion, rather than as a moral philosophy, is the acknowledged dependence of man upon an ultimate Way, the Tao. The supreme goal of religious life for Lao-tse, the founder of Taoism, is a knowledge of the eternal Tao. Knowledge of the Tao is conceived by some Taoists as union with it, and "on the road toward the union with Tao," says Chuang Tzu, a disciple of the founder of the faith, "the contemplating of the silent vastness of nature is of extreme importance."[18]

Although a contemplation of nature is essential to one type of Taoism, it is not essential to Taoism as a religion. Only a fraction of the vast number of Taoists think that contemplating nature is of primary importance in their religious life, because only a fraction of them are capable of contemplation. Thus it would be a mistake to identify a contemplation of nature with Taoism as a religion. What is of primary religious significance in Taoism is the reference beyond nature, and "the beauty of the universe" to "the principles of created things." It is this reference to a reality which is esteemed as more ultimate than nature itself which is the primary element in Taoism as a religion.

Religions of the world differ in interpretations of the nature of an ultimate reality, but all acknowledge that human life is dependent upon such a reality for the achievement of what is most to be desired. The most desired goal of life for the ancient Hindu writers of the Upanishads is union with the eternal Atman, the ultimate One. Religious life as interpreted in the Upanishads therefore includes all that men do to bring about the union of their individual atman with the ultimate Atman.

Such a union is one type of salvation, but since there are goals of religious life other than union with an ultimate reality, it would be indefensible to analyze salvation as a religious goal only in terms of union with an ultimate reality. Although man's relation to an ultimate reality is essential to all religious life, the particular relations of man to such a reality differ as religions differ.

Many religions stress union with an ultimate reality as the essence of salvation. The goal of religious life for the ancient Persians was union with Mithra, and the ritual of Mithraism was "planned to explain this goal and to indicate the steps by which the individual finally became one with (Mithra)."[19] The goal of religious life for the ancient Egyptian was to become one with Osiris, "the most renowned of Egypt's gods." Essential to this cult of Osiris was the faith that any man, whether he be commoner or king, may after death be identified with Osiris. The faith of all who worshiped Osiris as the supreme god is that Osiris does not die, and therefore all who trust in him will likewise "not see corruption," but "shall live," and "shall wake up in peace."

The anticipation of a conscious life after death is essential to the cult of Osiris, but it is not essential to all religious faith. For the Hindu whose faith is expressed in the Upanishads, the life after death will not be conscious. Believing that the supremely desirable goal of life is to relinquish all that separates him from his eternal source, the Hindu looks forward to his salvation as a loss of his identity in the eternal One.

The "aim and promise of the Dionysian rites" is "union with Dionysos, the God of life and the master of death."[20] What is peculiar to this cult is what is believed to be appropriate for man to do to bring himself into relation with the ultimate source of his salvation. What is not peculiar to it as a religious faith is the conviction that there is an ultimate reality upon which man is finally dependent for the achievement of all he most cherishes. Entering into a relation with his god is also the religious objective of the Navaho, who expresses his desire in the *Mountain Song* of the *Night Chant*: "In a holy place with a god I walk . . . In old age wandering with a god I walk. On a trail of beauty with a god I walk."[21] The Papuan of New Guinea devoutly makes a mask of Kovave, his god, and in the initiation ritual, places this mask over his own head, believing that "he is within the god, and the god is round about him, and they are somehow one."[22] "Wearing the mask of the kachina," the Zuni believes that he "becomes the very supernatural being he represents." For him, "the mask is the corporeal substance of the kachina, and in putting it on . . . (he) assumes the personality of the god."[23]

Although it may well be, as Professor Albright maintains, that "so far as we can judge, . . . the experiences of religious . . . mystical union with God are unknown in the ancient Near East outside of Israel,"[24] it would be a mistake, in the light of anthropological data, to assume that an experience is peculiar to any one religion, or to any one religious tradition.

Essential to all religious life is the faith that there is an ultimate reality, in relation to which alone man can achieve the supremely desired goal of his life. Union with this reality by means of ritual, in which individuals reverently employ the symbol of their god in the form of a mask, is for some primitive people their religion. Their religion obviously does not include the meditative contemplation of the universe as does the religion of the mystic Taoist, and it does not include the monistic metaphysic of an ultimate reality as does the Hindu faith expressed in the Upanishads. It does, however, include an earnest turning beyond man himself and beyond his resources to a reality he reveres as the ultimate determiner of all that he most cherishes.

4. *Religious life includes every aspect of an individual's acknowledgment of his dependence upon an ultimate reality*

An awareness of dependence, although essential to religious life, is not the only aspect of religious life. No awareness of dependence would even be a religious experience without an acknowledgment of dependence upon a reality revered as the ultimate determiner of all that an individual cherishes. Schleiermacher, therefore, for one, made a mistake in analyzing religion as the feeling of absolute dependence."[25] A feeling of absolute dependence is no more *the* religious experience than is an acknowledgment of dependence *the* religious experience.

Religious experience occurs as a type of human life only when man is aware of his status in relation to two realities: one which confronts him with his dependent nature, and another which he trusts for a supplementation of his dependent nature. Any reality in relation to which man is made aware of the limits of his resources may thus become religiously significant. But an awareness of the limits of man's capacities to fulfill his own requirements is not, as such, religious experience. It is simply one element in an occasion for religious life.

Human life is religious only when it turns beyond itself and its resources to acknowledge that there is another reality which is more dependable. Only then is the feeling of dependence a religious experience. It is religious by virtue of what man does to acknowledge his insufficiency in relation to a reality he trusts for its dependability to supplement his insufficient life.

The feeling of dependence as such is not uniquely religious, no matter how acute the sense of dependence may be. An individual, for example, confronted by a tidal wave, capable of demolishing his home and destroying himself and his family, may be as aware of his helplessness as any human being could possibly be. But such a feeling of helplessness is not itself a religious experience. It is, however, an element in religious experience when an individual, who is aware of his helplessness, turns to a reality transcendent of his life and his resources, because he trusts it to do for him what his own resources cannot do. It is this turning beyond man's life to a reality trusted for its contribution to his life that makes life religious; and every aspect of man's life which is involved in this turning to a reality trusted for its ultimate dependability is religiously significant.

Every experience, whether it be fear or hope, anxiety or confidence, is an element in religious life when it is included in the total pattern of a life which turns with trust beyond itself to a reality capable of doing for it in its need what no other reality can do for it. No experience, therefore, would be religious apart from what man does to relate himself to a reality he trusts more than any other reality, because he reveres it for its supreme dependability. Schleiermacher is certainly to be commended for stressing the feeling of complete dependence, yet his analysis is deficient because of its oversimplification. Feeling is one element in religious life, but it is only one element in a complex human response in which man acknowledges both his dependent status, and also his relation to a reality upon which he depends.

An emphasis on a feeling of dependence, therefore, is not an adequate analysis of either religious experience or religious faith in a reality transcendent of human life. Yet this is what Schleiermacher proposed to do when he maintained that the beliefs of a religious individual are interpretations of his feeling of absolute dependence. Schleiermacher's procedure is understandable, however, when one considers his premise. He believed that religious life is not a matter of doctrine and dogma, which are concepts, but is rather an experience which is not derived from concepts. That this analysis is in part defensible must be admitted, even when it is criticized. It is necessary to point out, as Schleiermacher does, that religious experience is the innermost nature of a person's life, and therefore, in the terminology of this essay, is a type of life. As such, it is neither an understanding of a concept, nor the ability to articulate a dogma. But even though religious life is not an intellectual comprehension of ideas, nevertheless, a clear understanding of man's status in relation to a reality transcendent of human life and the physical world is essential to religious life. Thus a feeling of dependence is religious only when man is clearly aware that in his dependent status he is in relation to a reality which is dependable, and which is accessible to him in his need when he turns to it in a way which is appropriate for receiving its help.

What man believes is an appropriate condition for receiving its help is his interpretation of his responsibilities in relation to it, and without such an interpretation, there is no religious life. Religious life includes all that man believes is worthy for acknowledging his final dependence upon an ultimate reality he reveres and trusts as supremely dependable. The faith of a religious individual, therefore, is not an interpretation of experience, even though it be "the feeling of absolute dependence."

A Hindu, with a developed philosophical mentality, is religious, therefore, for the same reason that a primitive Ainu is religious. It is because of his devout acknowledgment that he is ultimately dependent upon a supremely dependable reality, transcendent of human resources and of the physical world. The meditative mystics of Hinduism, Buddhism, and Taoism contemplate the eternal Atman, the eternal Dharma, and the eternal Tao, but all alike revere an ultimate reality in relation to which they reverently acknowledge their dependence for the achievement of what they most cherish. For the mystic Hindu this is a resolution of his soul, or atman, into the eternal Soul, or ultimate Atman. For the contemplative Buddhist, it is an attainment of Nirvana, made possible by knowing the eternal Dharma, and by conforming to it as the final authority for his enlightened life. For the philosophical Taoist, it is an identification of his life with the universe, through which he comes to discover its eternal principle, the Tao, which thereby becomes the ultimate law for his life.

Religious experience is one type of consciousness, but it is specifically the consciousness of a reality transcendent of human life and the physical world upon which man acknowledges his final dependence. It is one type of feeling of dependence but it is specifically the feeling of dependence upon a reality which man trusts as dependable and to which he turns for its indispensable contribution to his life. Underlying religious faith, therefore, is always the conviction that whatever is less than the Ultimate is less than completely dependable.

Chapter Three

THE METAPHYSIC OF RELIGIOUS LIFE

When "metaphysic" is defined as an interpretation of the nature of an ultimate reality, it is clear that some metaphysic is essential to religious life. Any interpretation of the nature of a reality believed to be ultimate is a metaphysic, whether the interpretation is that of an individual who lives in a primitive culture, or of one who lives in a civilized culture. Man's effort to interpret the nature of the total context in which he lives is not confined to any one type of culture. It is, however, possible for man to interpret the nature of an ultimate reality without also doing all that he believes it is worthy of him to do in acknowledging his dependence upon it. Hence religion is not simply an aspect of metaphysics.

1. *Religious life includes an interpretation of a reality believed to be transcendent of human life and all its resources*

There are at least two beliefs included in every interpretation underlying religious life. One is that a reality exists transcendent of human life and the physical world. The other is that this reality is of supreme significance for human life. Without these two judgments of existence and of value, there is no religious life. Religious life, however, is not merely a judgment about the significance of an ultimate reality for human life. It is rather the earnest effort to do all that man believes is worthy of him to do in acknowledging his dependence upon it.

There is a fundamental difference between a value judgment and a religious adjustment. A value judgment is simply an estimate of the significance of a reality for human life. When such an acknowledged significance motivates an individual to orient his life to the valued reality, his behavior is an adjustment. It is specifically a religious adjustment when the valued reality is interpreted as an ultimate reality, having a significance for human life which is supreme above all other realities.

Even though a reality is believed to be ultimate, a belief about its ultimate nature is not uniquely religious. A belief about an ultimate reality is religious only when it constitutes a basis for a reverent acknowledgment of man's ultimate dependence. A metaphysical belief, therefore, has religious significance only when man does all that he can do to revere the reality he regards as ultimate.

Just as there is no religion without some adjustment to a reality revered as ultimate, so there is no religion without a metaphysic. But the metaphysic which is essential to religious life is not conditioned by the peculiarities of a culture. Although a culture conditions the specific way in which a person expresses his understanding of reality, no peculiarity of culture is essential for the religious belief itself that there is a reality of supreme importance for human life which is transcendent of human resources.

(a) *The basic motive for a religious life is not self-centered*

Religious life is a reverence for a reality which man esteems as supreme in significance above every other reality, and so religious life cannot be analyzed in the concepts of a hedonistic philosophy. A hedonistic analysis of human motivation rests upon the assumption that there is one motive underlying human life, and that is to acquire a benefit for one's own life. When this motive is affirmed as the only motivation of human life, there is, of course, no way to escape the conclusion that religious behavior expresses a self-centered concern. This conclusion follows because it is only another way of stating the premise with which human motivation is interpreted. But with this self-centered preoccupation, there is no way to account for some of the characteristic features of religious life, such as an acknowledgment of man's subordination to the reality he esteems as ultimate.

A religious individual, irrespective of his cultural opportunities, reveres as best he can the reality he regards as ultimate. His frequent failure to accomplish what he undertakes to do does not discredit his motive. It constitutes merely a disparity between what he proposes to accomplish and what he actually accomplishes. Yet, when any individual believes that there is an ultimate reality which has a significance for his life which no other reality has, his metaphysic, insofar as it is limited to this belief, is not conditioned by the peculiarities of his culture, and it is this belief which is basic to all religious life.

Religious life does not presuppose a knowledge of an ultimate reality, but rather an earnest desire to know such a reality. Knowledge is information, and a knowledge of an ultimate reality would be an informed interpretation of an ultimate reality. Such an interpretation is the objective of religious life, even when the objective is not attained. An essential motive of religious life is to understand the nature of the ultimate reality, in order that man may do all he believes he ought to do to revere it for its supreme significance in his life. That this reality is believed to have ultimate control over human life, and therefore is believed to be the final determiner of human well-being, ought not, however, to assume such an emphasis in an interpretation of religion that religious life is regarded as an aspect of hedonism.

Hedonism is a point of view that what is contributory to one's well-being is alone of utmost significance for him. According to this point of view, the basic motive of human life is to achieve well-being for one's self, and for others insofar as their well-being contributes to one's own. This, however, is not the primary motive of religious life. The primary motive of religious life is to do all that is believed to be worthy for acknowledging with reverence the reality upon which man believes he is ultimately dependent for his life.

Man is concerned with his life, but a differentiation of religion and morality rests upon what man considers to be of pre-eminent significance for his life. If his own well-being is his sole preoccupation, he is not religious. He is religious, however, when in the achievement of his well-being he is motivated reverently to take into account his relationship to a reality upon which he acknowledges his final dependence, and which he esteems above all else.

The first concern of religious life is to do all that an individual believes is worthy of himself in his relationship to a reality whose significance he acknowledges as supreme over all other realities. To interpret religious motivation, therefore, as basically a hedonistic preoccupation with an individual's own well-being is a distortion of a vast amount of the data of human history. The presumption that all human motivation can be accounted for in terms of a hedonistic concern is a bias with which religious life is often interpreted, but it is an indefensible bias. Its classification as a "bias" does not necessarily disparage it as a point of view. Any point of view which underlies an interpretation is a bias. The ground, however, for disparaging the hedonistic bias for interpreting religious life is its inability to account for data traditionally included in the category of religion.

Religion includes all that men do to revere a reality for its pre-eminent status in existence, and so for its supreme importance in human life. This order of existence and value may not be reversed. A reality is not believed to be ultimate in existence because it is cherished for its utmost significance in life. Rather, its pre-eminent importance in life is its status as the ultimate determiner of life.

(b) *The basic motive of religious faith is to orient life to the reality esteemed as ultimate*

There is no religious life without some belief about the nature of a reality to which man is related as ultimately dependent. Hence there is no religious experience before there is an acknowledgment of man's dependence upon a reality other than himself which he esteems for its pre-eminent importance. A belief in the pre-eminent status of one reality in distinction to all others is an essential feature of religious life, and therefore it is a primary feature of a religious metaphysic. This order, however, is denied by every philosopher who begins his analysis of religious life from the point of view that feeling is the fundamental basis of religious life. Schleiermacher, for example, popularized this point of view when he maintained that the feeling of absolute dependence is the primary religious experience, secondary to which are all the beliefs of religious life. This point of view is also defended by Professor Wobbermin when he maintains that "in relegating religion to the realm of feeling, Schleiermacher was and still remains correct."

Implied in the point of view that feeling is the primary basis of religious life is the idea that feeling may be religiously significant in an individual's life even before the individual has any belief. In a very artificial scheme for classifying the aspects of religious life, Professor Wobbermin proposes that the so-called first "stratum" of religious life is "religious experience," and the second stratum is "the religious conviction." The point of view maintained in this essay, on the other hand, is that a religious feeling of dependence is man's response to a reality he believes exists transcendent of himself. This feeling is not the source from which the belief is derived that there is a reality transcendent of human life. A belief essential to the religious feeling of dependence is that there is a reality transcendent of human life and the physical world upon which man is ultimately dependent, and religious life includes all that man does to relate himself to this reality he believes is ultimate, and worthy to be worshiped for its pre-eminent status in existence. Its pre-eminent status in existence is the assumed basis for its supreme significance in religious life, and religious life includes all that a man specifically does to revere it for its supreme significance.

When feeling is regarded as the primary aspect of religious life, religious belief is regarded as secondary to feeling. When this order of feeling and belief is maintained in a philosophy of religion, a feature of feeling is looked upon as the primary clue to the nature of religious life. According to Professor Wobbermin, "it is the uncertainty of feeling that determines the nature of religion."[1] Implied in this point of view is an analysis of religious life which does not take into account man's acknowledgment of his relation to a reality he regards as supremely worthy of his reverence. In declaring that "feeling is given without an object," Wobbermin explicitly maintains that religious life is possible without any acknowledgment of a reality of supreme significance before which man is subordinate and upon which he is dependent. Wobbermin's analysis is consistent with his anti-rationalistic polemic, but his bias is incapable of analyzing the data of human history which is traditionally classified as religious.

Included in religious life is the belief that men are confronted by a reality transcendent of themselves which is ultimate in the order of existence. This belief which is basic to religious life may be embellished and developed into a theological system, but when it is expanded into such a system, it is merely clarified. The belief is fundamentally the same whether it is maintained by a primitive individual or by a philosophically trained theologian. Its embellishment into a metaphysical system, however, constitutes an obvious difference between the set of ideas of primitive men and the highly developed set of ideas of trained philosophers. But this difference is not primarily of religious signficance. What is of primary religious significance is the conviction that there is a reality upon which man is ultimately dependent, and which is supremely worthy of his reverence.

The set of beliefs which constitutes a primitive equivalent for a developed metaphysic in a civilized culture is, as Aristotle says, "like one who lisps, since it is young and in its beginnings."[2] But lisping after all is not a feature of beliefs. It is rather a peculiarity of their articulation. And peculiarities of articulation, just as peculiarities of the formulation of beliefs into systems, are not essential to religious life. They are earmarks of a particular culture; not of a primary faith basic to all religious life.

2. *The reality to which a religious adjustment is made may be interpreted as a power*

A primary belief in the religious life of primitive people is that there is a "power" other than the objects which make up the totality of the physical world. Although an interpretation of this power is not developed by primitive men into any set of consistent ideas, the belief that this power has supreme significance for human life is basic to primitive religious life. An acknowledgment of its significance for human life is expressed in all that primitive men do in their rituals and ceremonials to revere it and to respect it.

Primitive men's acknowledgment that they are dependent upon a reality they esteem as ultimate in importance in their life is not an interpretation of their experience. Their belief that there is such a power which confronts them is an interpretation of a reality other than their experience, although their belief that there is a reality other than their experience has its basis in events of which they are aware in their experience.

A tree, for example, which falls upon the dwelling of a primitive person, reveals a power over his life which is not a feature of his life. The power over his life is a feature of a reality which makes an impact upon his life. Every object in the context in which man lives makes an impact upon his life in one way or another, but only the objects of which man is aware because of their special significance in his life are religiously significant. The religious significance of a reality rests upon its utmost importance for human life, although its significance in man's life is not necessarily a product of his life.

Anything which becomes an object of attention has a significance because of the attention it attracts. When, however, its capacity to attract attention is stressed as an explanation for the attention which man directs to it, its significance in man's life is not accounted for as a feature of his life. Its significance for him is explained rather as a feature of its nature in relation to his life.

These two fundamentally different theories of value are implied in two fundamentally different theories of reality. One theory of reality is that every object which is significant for man is given its significance by man. The other theory is that objects which are significant in man's life have a nature which in part explains their significance in his life.

It must be acknowledged that many objects have a significance for man purely as a result of his peculiar way of regarding them. But it would be pressing a sound point of view too far to maintain that every reality which is significant in man's life has such significance because of man's peculiar response to it, rather than because of its impact upon him. An interpretation of all religiously significant realities as projections is a result of a philosophical bias that all value estimates are human distinctions, and as human distinctions, are experiences, the bases for which are peculiarities of an individual.

Value-distinctions and value-judgments are experiences. Hence it is permissible to interpret the nature of value-distinctions and value-judgments as features of an individual's life. But it is indefensible to maintain that the sole basis for every value distinction is experience. A tree, for example, which falls on a native's hut is not a product of his experience, and its significance for him as destructive of what he cherishes is likewise not a product of his experience.

The attempt, therefore, to interpret all significance for human life as derived solely from man's experience is indefensible. An individual may value many things by virtue of the peculiarities of his experience. Yet, there are other realities, and man's estimate of their significance in his life may express his understanding of their nature in relation to his life.

There are many realities which make impacts upon man either for his benefit or for his harm, and these impacts have nothing whatever to do with his responses. The capacity of a tree to demolish a dwelling is a feature of a tree in relation to a dwelling capable of being destroyed. Any person with intelligence enough to distinguish his dwelling from a tree which falls on it is intelligent enough to recognize the capacity of the tree to destroy his dwelling. And such capacity to destroy is not projected.

An animal capable of killing a defenseless individual has a capacity which is not ascribed to it by the individual who fears it. Its capacity to injure is its nature, and an individual's fear of it is a response informed by a very clear understanding of its nature. It is, therefore, inexcusable to interpret every event in which man is confronted by the alternative of life or death as an instance of projection. It is likewise inexcusable to maintain that every reality which is feared has a capacity to destroy only insofar as it is feared. This type of philosophy, while perfectly intelligible, is thoroughly indefensible when confronted by the data with which men are confronted. Every human being is capable of being destroyed by some reality, and whatever has this capacity to destroy has a significance for human life which is not ascribed to it. Thus it is indefensible to maintain that all realities which are religiously significant for primitive men have a power ascribed to them by primitive men. It is undeniable that there are many realities which primitive men fear as a result of their ignorance. But it is also undeniable that there are other realities which are feared because they are understood.

After primitive men have done all that they can to protect themselves by means of their implements, they are still confronted by the danger of wild animals. After they have taken all the precautions of which they are capable, they are still subject to diseases. It is this capacity of things to put human life into jeopardy and to imperil its well-being which impresses all men, civilized no less than primitive. Whatever these realities may be, whether animals or diseases, tidal waves or avalanches of snow, floods or droughts, all men who are confronted by them are made aware of their relation to realities other than themselves over which they do not have final control.

The interpretation of such realities as "powers" is, to be sure, a peculiarity of human experience. But the fact that there are such realities which have the capacity to destroy men is not a peculiarity of human experience. It is peculiar to some primitive cultures to refer to such powers as instances of "mana," but the term "mana" as a primitive language term is something very different from the reality it is intended to designate. Mana for the primitive is a power other than himself which is capable of affecting his life, and his belief about such a power is the sense of his term "mana."[3]

Hence it is purely arbitrary to emphasize primitive man's interpretation as the sole significance of his symbol "mana." The symbol as such is a man-made sign, but its sense is the destructive or beneficial nature of certain realities in relation to which man lives. These realities which affect his well-being are not just his interpretations, and their significance for his life is not a product of his symbolism. His symbolism is simply one means by which he takes their significance into account, and by means of which he differentiates them from other realities which do not have comparable significance for his life.

There are many terms in the vocabularies of primitive peoples for designating a reality which is the object of their religious adjustment. "Mana" for the Melanesians designates a power believed to be present in many objects, and in whatever object it is believed to be present, it constitutes the occasion for their special attention. Hence the religion of this primitive people consists of the special attention given to objects believed to possess mana.

Vague and diffuse as this power may be which they both fear and respect, it is the supremely significant referent of their religious life. Believed to be other than all physical objects, it is likewise believed to be other than their possessions. When they regard it as other than all physical objects, and so other than their possessions, they interpret it with an attribute essential to every religious metaphysic.

The type of reality which the Melanesians designate by the term "mana" is designated by the aboriginal Arunta of Australia with the term "arung quilta." This same type of reality is named "dzo" by the West African tribes;[4] "orenda" by the Red Indian Iroquois; "manitou" by the Algonquins; "wakanada" by the Sioux. According to the belief of all of these primitive people, there is a reality other than the physical objects they control, which they both fear and respect, and it is feared for the harm it can do to them when they do not respect it as they believe it ought to be respected.

The motive for many of the rituals of primitive people is to safeguard themselves from the harmful effect of a reality regarded as a power. The emphasis by the Arunta upon its destructive character so predominates its beneficial role that for them it "seems always to work in a harmful way."[5] This interpretation characteristic of the religious life of the Arunta is easily understood. The poverty of their life gives little occasion for them to believe that there is any reality working for their well-being. The hardships of their life in the struggle for sheer survival undoubtedly condition what they believe about the world in which they live. This world, for them, is not a manifestation of beneficent power. Yet, the aspect of their life which is religious includes all they do to take an unfriendly power into account. The basic motive of their religious behavior is to control it so as to reduce, as far as they are able, its unfavorable impact upon their life.

The margin between religion and magic for this primitive people is tenuous, just as it is for many people who do not live in a culture equally primitive. What any people do in relation to a reality is religious, rather than magical, insofar as they acknowledge that it cannot be controlled by anything they possess. Insofar, however, as they believe that they possess the means to control it, their point of view is not religious, but is the point of view underlying all magic. When the Arunta acknowledge that after they have used every means they possess to influence this power, there is still a surplus power which they cannot directly control, and before which they are totally dependent, their point of view shares a feature in common with all religious life. It is this qualification of their confidence in their own capacities to control the power they call "arung quilta" which distinguishes their magic from their religion.

In common to both religion and magic is the acknowledgment of a reality other than human possessions, of such a character that it must seriously be taken into account. Yet the means by which it is taken into account differ because the point of view of men toward it differs. If men believe that they can control this reality transcendent of their possessions by devices which they possess, their point of view is not religious, but is characteristic of a belief in magic. Although this distinction between religion and magic is clear as a definition, it is not so clear for many people who use ritual to control a reality they believe to be transcendent of themselves and which they believe has a capacity either to harm or to benefit them.

Although rituals may be used with a confidence characteristic of magic, man's point of view is religious when he acknowledges that there is a reality he cannot completely control by his ritual, and therefore before which he is dependent.

The inclination to trust in ritual, rather than in a reality to which it refers, constitutes a universal temptation. It is not only individuals who live in a primitive culture who succumb to this temptation. People with the mentality of primitives who live in civilized cultures also do. The Canaanites, for example, believed there are powers transcendent of the physical world which ultimately determine their lives, and they employed two terms for designating these powers. One is "el," and the other "baal." Since the manifestations of el were many, the Canaanites believed there were many such powers, and so they referred to el in the plural, using the term "elim" or "elohim." Since the power called "baal" likewise was manifested in many ways, they referred to it by the plural term "bealim."[6]

The differentiation of a primitive culture and a civilized culture is clear even though the superficial differences are many. The distinction is not so clear between the mentality of a primitive individual who lives in a primitive culture and an individual with a primitive mentality who lives in a civilized culture. The difficulty in making this distinction is due to the superficial gloss which partially conceals a primitive mentality when it occurs in a civilized setting. When, however, the basic point of view of individuals is clearly understood, the difference between primitive mentality and civilized mentality is not so radical as are the differences in the equipment which primitive and civilized men use.

One part of such equipment is symbolic. When symbols in civilized culture are used with the same point of view as they are used in primitive cultures, their sense is the same. This basic identity in the sense of symbols, whether they are language terms or ritualistic acts, is a matter of a fundamental similarity in mentality. When a ritual is regarded as capable of controlling a reality of utmost significance in man's life, it is motivated by a point of view shared by all who believe in magic.

Ritual may also be used by one individual with the point of view basic to magic and also with the point of view basic to religion. This fusion of two radically different points of view into one person's mentality is illustrated in Hindu culture. "Brahman," for example, is a term with which the ultimate reality is designated, but it is also a term for designating "a vague, semi-magical power ascribed by the priesthood, particularly in connection with the sacrifices."[7] When the same term is used to designate two fundamentally different realities, it would be indefensible to infer from a particular instance of its use specifically what the term is intended to designate. The same term "Brahman" refers both to a reality over which man believes he has final control, and also to a reality over which he acknowledges he does not have final control.

Although the term is the same, its symbolic roles are radically different. It is, therefore, not always possible for an observer of another person's life to ascertain which of his symbols perform a religious role and which perform a magical role. It is not always possible to ascertain this because the distinction is a matter of the attitude of an individual toward the role of the symbol he uses. When a ritual, for example, is regarded as a device for controlling a reality believed to be of utmost significance for man's life, it is used with the attitude of one who trusts in his possessions as the final determinant of what he supremely values. It is then a magical device, because it is trusted for what it can do to achieve what otherwise could not be achieved without it. Man possesses the ritual, and if he believes he can accomplish all he supremely desires by means of it alone, he then believes that he has final control over all that he cherishes.

The point of view toward ritual which is characteristic of magic is fundamentally incompatible with religious faith. Ritual in religious life performs a symbolic role. For one who believes in magic, it does not. Any individual, therefore, primitive or civilized, who forgets that he is ultimately dependent upon a reality before which he is always subordinate, also forgets that his ritual is his own creation. When, however, ritual which man creates is used to acknowledge his ultimate dependence upon a reality to which it refers, it performs a religious function. Its religious function is its specific symbolic reference to a reality believed to be transcendent of all human possessions, and so transcendent of every reality which is directly under man's control.

The Chinese term "Te" designates a power which is believed to be manifested in many particular things of importance in human life.[8] This power in particular things is religiously significant for the Chinese when they acknowledge their final subordination to it, and their ultimate dependence upon it. But when they believe they can manipulate it by means of their ritualistic devices, it is not religiously significant. A reality which can be manipulated by man is within man's control, and a reality which is within man's control is not the ultimate reality revered by religious life.

One cannot infer the specific sense of the Chinese symbol "Te" from its particular uses. Its sense is its significance for the individual who uses the term, and this term can be used with two radically different senses, just as the term "Brahman" can be used. A religious individual uses the same symbols as does a non-religious individual, but he uses them for different functions, and so with different senses. The function of the symbol "Brahman" for a religious Hindu designates the ultimate reality upon which every derivative reality is acknowledged to depend, but the same term may be used as a device assumed to possess magical potency, efficacious for securing a particular good which man desires. As efficacious for securing a desired good, its role is not symbolic. It is an implement which is used for its leverage over another reality. It does not refer beyond itself to a reality other than itself. It operates upon such a reality.

Any object may perform a religious function, just as it may perform a magical function. The difference in function, however, is not a feature of an object. It is a feature of the mentality of an individual who uses the object. When an object is used as a means for acknowledging a reality which man reveres as supreme in significance above every other reality, it performs the role of a sign in his religious life. The religious role performed by a sign is, therefore, not a property of the sign. The way it is used determines its significance. An object may be used in almost any way man chooses, but the way he chooses makes a fundamental difference in the nature of its significance for his life.

For example, the differentiation sign is a symbol used in the priestly robes of Chinese Emperors. According to Dr. Ackerman, it refers to "the crescent and decrescent moon" as a means for acknowledging "the Power in the waxing and re-waxing moon." When this symbol refers to a power which is revered for its ultimate control over the growth of man's crops, it has religious significance, and the acknowledged significance of this "growth-energy" for human life is the religious sense of this symbol. This symbol, therefore, performs a religious role on imperial priestly robes when it is used to designate a reality of supreme importance upon which man acknowledges his ultimate dependence.

This symbol, however, has the unlimited adaptability of all man-made devices. When it is used as a means for controlling the "growth-energy" believed to be related to "the self-regenerating cycle of the moon,"[9] it has a significance peculiar to individuals who trust in magic, since a trust in magic is basically a confidence in the ultimate sufficiency of man's own resources.

Confidence in the complete sufficiency of man's resources is, however, incompatible with religious life. When religious individuals use a symbol, it is not any presumed efficacy of the symbol which they trust. The role of a religiously significant symbol for them is its reference to the ultimate source upon which they depend for the goods they most need.

What men believe they most need conditions what they seek, and what they seek as the most desired of all goods determines the sense of their religious symbols. As a symbol for a reality of supreme importance, the primitive Melanesians use the term "mana," and the manifestations of mana with which they are concerned consequently determine the type of object they select for referring to it.

The most impressive power for many people throughout the world is the vitality underlying the growth of crops, of cattle, and of people. This accounts for the widespread use of phallic symbols. When, however, a phallic representation becomes an object with which people are preoccupied, it loses its symbolic function. Rather than referring to a fertility power of the soil, of cattle, and of people, it becomes the object of their attention, and when attention is focused upon an object so that it does not direct an individual beyond it, it does not perform a sign function.

Any object may perform the role of a sign for one individual, and not for another. For this reason, it is impossible to ascertain which object performs a symbolic function, and which does not, unless one can ascertain the particular type of mentality which is associated with the use of a particular object. When an object does not direct an individual beyond it, but is itself the object of his exclusive preoccupation, it is not a sign. As such it cannot be religiously significant. And conversely, no matter what the object may be which directs an individual beyond itself to a reality upon which he reverently acknowledges his ultimate dependence, the object is religiously significant as a sign. Thus even phallic representations may conceivably perform a religious function when they refer to a reality believed to be the ultimate determinant of the productivity of land, of cattle, and of people. The use of a phallic representation, therefore, should not necessarily be disparaged as unworthy of a religious function. What is unworthy of religious function of any object is its tendency to constrict an individual's attention to itself.

When a representation does not direct an individual beyond itself, it does not perform a symbolic role, and so it is unsatisfactory for religious use. This tendency to constrict attention to itself is not peculiar to a phallic representation. It is universal to every object. Every conceivable object may become the focus of attention, and when attention is constricted to an object in man's possession so that it does not refer an individual beyond it, it is a handicap to his religious life. The handicap to religious life in the use of phallic representations is, therefore, not for conventional moral reasons. It is for a basic principle of symbolism. When attention is restricted to a phallic representation, the representation does not perform a symbolic function. But when a phallic representation refers to a reality revered for its ultimate significance over the productivity of the soil, of animals, and of human beings, there is then no basic reason for denying its religious significance.

The religious function of any representation is its referential role—its reference to a reality upon which man acknowledges his ultimate dependence. When an individual is not directed beyond a representation to a reality upon which he acknowledges his final dependence, the representation is not symbolic, and therefore its role in his life is not religious. When attention is centered on the "organs of sex," it is indefensible to classify phallicism as a "mode of the worship of

Fertility."[10] The fact that a preoccupation with phallic representations is universal, ought not to be carelessly interpreted as a "mode of worship." Worship is a reference of human life beyond human life. When any aspect of human life, or any part of man's possessions, becomes the focus of attention, beyond which an individual does not turn to acknowledge his ultimate dependence, there is no religion, and so there is no specifically religious worship.

This distinction between representations which may be religiously significant, and those which are not, is not arbitrary. It is a matter of a fundamental principle of the function of representations. When a representation which man makes does not direct attention beyond itself, but becomes an object with which he is exclusively preoccupied, it is not a symbol. Hence the difference between an object which is a symbol, and one which is not a symbol, is not a feature of an object. It is rather the role it assumes in the life of an individual. And this role is a peculiarity of an individual's mentality.

When the latitude of life is restricted to any elementary aspect, whether it is food or sex, the scope of an individual's life is correspondingly confined to objects which are immediately related to his animal interests.[11] But this particular effect has nothing essentially to do with religion, even with primitive religion. The inheritances from animal ancestry constitute the most elementary interests of human life, and when human life is reduced to the scope of an animal's concerns, most objects lose all symbolic significance. They lose this significance when the horizon of life is no wider than the objects which immediately contribute to the most insistent of desires.

The function of a symbol is to mediate, or to go between an individual and a reality to which it directs his attention. When an object does not perform this mediating function, it is not a symbol, and no matter what the object may be, it is not an element in religious life.

The ability of primitive men to acknowledge a "power in all productive things . . . in the fruitful soil . . . (in) cattle and in the human family,"[12] is a capacity basic to primitive religious life. When the productivity of the soil directs man's attention to a reality upon which he acknowledges its productivity to be ultimately dependent, he interprets the productivity of the soil as a sign of a reality other than it. When the birth of life directs his attention to a reality acknowledged to be ultimately determinative of life, he interprets life from the point of view of one capable of distinguishing an instance of life from a condition upon which all life ultimately depends.

It was an achievement of utmost importance for early man to distinguish between the soil and the fertility-character of the soil, just as it was to distinguish between animals and the fertility-character of animal life. This achievement of human mentality is a condition for man's spiritual life, one aspect of which is his religious life. A feature of spiritual life is its capacity to extend the scope of human interests, and when this scope extends to comprehend the ultimate reality upon which man acknowledges his final dependence, spiritual life becomes religious life.

Religious life is an aspect of spiritual life, and therefore without some spiritual life there is no religious life. There are, however, many degrees of spiritual life. Yet, common to all of them is the capacity to refer beyond a particular thing to another reality. In this reference of one object to another, the scope of life enlarges, and the extent of its scope is determined by the character of the reality to which reference is made as the Ultimate.

When a symbol for the Ultimate is copied from one of man's possessions, the significance of the symbol is also borrowed from the associations which man makes with his own possessions. One of the profound misfortunes of human life is that its symbols are often inadequate for the distinctions of which it is spiritually capable. Capable, for example, as were the ancient Canaanites of distinguishing a god of the earth from the earth itself, they were insufficiently cautious in selecting the symbols for designating it. Although they acknowledged their ultimate dependence upon "the patriarch El—the Numen par excellence," they represented El with a symbol no more august than the figure of a bull, and hence for them, " 'Bull' was one of his standard titles."[13]

3. *The reality to which religious adjustment is made may be interpreted as living*

There are many evidences of primitive man's awareness that he is confronted by a reality which has utmost significance for his life. Artifacts as ancient as paleolithic culture indicate that men endeavored to take into account some reality other than their own possessions. This reality was conceived as significant for their lives, and so was acknowledged as having influence or power over their lives. Thus it is easy to understand why it was interpreted as a living power. The fact, for example, that falling trees injure men and destroy their dwellings may well have been taken as an indication that trees, like men themselves have a "life-power."

The belief of early men in some power in things which move, or some form of life-power, may be classified as a vitalism. It is a vitalism in the sense that movements of bodies are regarded as manifestations of a factor other than the bodies themselves. This vitalistic point of view is not peculiar to primitive cultures. It is basic to Aristotle's biology, just as it is basic to the philosophies of Hans Driesch and other modern thinkers who have endeavored to interpret the nature of living things.

The distinction, however, between animate and inanimate objects is not clear for primitive men. Hence for them, the idea of a living power explains to their satisfaction the movements of all bodies. Although a primitive interpretation of moving bodies does not rest upon a distinct idea of a life-force, or a living principle immanent in moving bodies, it does rest upon a distinction between a physical body and a factor other than it which moves it. A body which does not move is predictable, but a body which is capable of moving is not predictable, and according to primitive men, this is because there is a cause for its movement which is other than the body itself.

Primitive men cannot predict when trees will be uprooted by storms, or when their huts will be demolished by winds, or when their crops will be destroyed by rain. Their inability to predict the many occurrences which affect their lives is not, however, unique to their primitive culture. It is a feature of human life. In spite of the techniques of modern meteorology, many occurrences are either not predictable, or when predicted cannot be controlled. The inability completely to understand and control the physical context in which men live is not peculiar to any historical era. At every age in human history, men are confronted by some form of violence in nature—floods, earthquakes, volcanic eruptions, lightning. These manifestations of destructive forces have naturally tempted men to try to interpret them. When men's understanding of their nature is not clear, the sense of the symbols which designate them is correspondingly indistinct. Primitive men do not understand the nature of the physical world in which they live. Therefore the senses of the symbols by means of which they refer to aspects of the physical world are likewise not clear. When a term in a primitive vocabulary has no sense more distinct than its denotative function for designating the capacity of an object for making an impact upon human life, it may be classified as an element in a rudimentary dynamistic philosophy. Terms in a primitive vocabulary for designating such power are "mana," "orenda," "wakanda," "dzo."

An interpretation of realities significant for human life constitutes either a philosophy or a science. Hence a rudimentary philosophy, as well as a rudimentary science, is not peculiar to a civilized culture. A systematic philosophy, however, and a science consisting of carefully verified interpretations, are the achievements of a civilized culture. But primitive men who venture some interpretation of the nature of realities with which they are confronted have a rudimentary philosophy and a rudimentary science. The philosophy and science of primitive men are as undeveloped as is every other aspect of their life. Yet, undeveloped though they are, they are as much a characteristic feature of their culture as is their religion.

A primitive interpretation of the movement of physical bodies as a manifestation of a life-power immanent in moving bodies is a primitive vitalistic philosophy or science. When such a life-power becomes more significant for a primitive person than the physical bodies which are moved by it, so that he endeavors to take it into account in a way distinct from the manner in which he treats the bodies which are moved by it, his vitalistic premise becomes the basis for his religious life, and his religious life includes everything that he does to take this reality into account.

A primitive philosophy of movement may be classified as a vitalism when the explanatory factor for movement is regarded as some form of life, or some factor in moving bodies which is other than the physical bodies themselves. This distinction is apparent to a primitive person who observes that a tree which at one time moves in a storm is motionless at another time. His endeavor to explain the basis for this distinction is his philosophy, and his science. But his specific endeavor to take this reality into account as a supremely significant factor in his life is the motive for his religion. Although the motive for philosophy and science, even in primitive life, is to understand, the motive for religion in primitive and civilized life alike is to do what men believe is appropriate in their relation to a reality they revere for its supreme significance as an ultimate determinant of their lives.

When a primitive individual's explanation for the movement of physical bodies is in terms of power, but not specifically in terms of a life-power, his philosophy may be classified as dynamism. According to the point of view of dynamism, movements of physical bodies are manifestations of a power, not necessarily living, which is other than bodies which move. According to both dynamism and vitalism there is a power, or a life-power, which is regarded as other than moving bodies which make an impact upon men, either for their benefit or for their harm. What primitive men do to acknowledge that their lives are ultimately dependent upon such power, or life-power, is their religion.

The term "dynamism" is derived from a Greek word for "power." Hence dynamism traditionally has been a doctrine about some type of power. Insofar as this term in the Greek philosophical vocabulary did not have a clear connotation, its role in Greek philosophy is not fundamentally different from its role in primitive philosophy. The indistinct sense of the term "power," and consequently the vague character of a dynamistic philosophy, are not features peculiar to any culture. They are expressions of man's limited ability to understand the nature of the world in which he lives. What all men understand, however, is that there is a reality which confronts them, one aspect of which is its force or power to benefit them or to harm them.

There is no way for an interpreter of primitive religion to ascertain whether the earliest human philosophy is a dynamism, a vitalism, or an animism. The most that may be said is that if dynamism was the earliest philosophy, then there was a stage in human history in which man's religion was an attempt to adjust to "power." If vitalism was the first philosophy, then the earliest expression of religious life was man's adjustment to a life-force which he distinguished from things which live and move. If this life-power was believed to be less diffuse than a life-power in things which move, but was interpreted as an individual life in things which move, then the earliest philosophy was an animism, and the earliest religion was man's attempt to take into account the supreme significance in his life of spirits or souls dwelling in things which move.

It is enough, however, to classify these points of view without presuming to be able to date their origin in human history. Such dating is impossible. What is possible, and therefore permissible in a study of the religions of mankind, is a differentiation of the points of view which constitute the premises underlying religions. Basic to every religion is a premise, in the sense of some interpretation of the nature of the context in which men live. But the possibility for clearly distinguishing premises as types of philosophy does not imply that such clear distinctions have any historical counterpart in human cultures. The presupposition that there is such a counterpart accounts, therefore, for the indefensible procedure among some anthropologists of regarding "dynamism" as the "first" type of philosophy, and for others, of regarding "animatism" as the first type. Still others think "animism" was first. It is impossible to know which type of interpretation is "first," even though there is some evidence for believing that some cultures are predominantly oriented to what is believed to be "power," and others are oriented more specifically to a "life-power," and still others to a "spirit" in things which move.

All of these philosophies may simultaneously be maintained by one people, or by one person, for there is no fundamental incompatibility in these several points of view. These points of view differ primarily in the specificity with which the reality is interpreted that is believed to account for movement. But movement is not understood by primitive men, and therefore there is no clear distinction in their philosophies between animate objects and inanimate objects. Any thing which moves is believed to have features in common with everything else that moves. For some primitive people, rolling stones are not fundamentally different from living things, such as animals or human beings. But insofar as moving objects have religious significance, primitive men do distinguish the object which moves and the factor which accounts for its movement.

A body which at one time moves, and at another time is at rest, is, from the primitive point of view, other than the factor which moves it. Although this distinction is made by every primitive person whose religious life is his attempt to take such a principle of movement into account, it is not peculiar to primitive culture. It is also basic to physical and metaphysical philosophies in civilized culture, as, for example, in the philosophy of Aristotle.

There is certainly a vast difference between the systematic development of Aristotle's *Physics* and *Metaphysics* and the inarticulate beliefs of primitive men. But the premise which is basic to the philosophical system of Aristotle is not fundamentally different from the premise which is basic to primitive dynamistic philosophies which distinguish bodies that move from the factor which accounts for their movement. A stone at rest, according to a primitive dynamist, is not the same reality as a stone in motion, and the difference is the factor which accounts for its motion.

When the distinction between a lifeless body and a living body becomes the basic analogy for a primitive person's interpretations of the nature of the physical world, primitive men maintain what may be classified as an animistic philosophy. The primitive natives of Guiana, for example, believe that the "whole world swarms with beings" and that they are "surrounded by a host of them." It is for this reason that the

Indian of Guiana fears to be alone without some means of protection. When he must go away from his campfire at night, he carries a fire-brand. The motive for equipping himself in this way is that he may be able to see "the beings among whom he moves." The primitive Bantu of Africa believes that "spirits dwell in springs, rivers, and lakes, in rocks and piles of stone, in trees, caves and hills."[14] Since he cannot see them, he assumes that they move when he does not see them. Whatever occurs in his environment which he cannot account for in any other way, he accounts for in terms of such spirits.

This way of accounting for occurrences is not peculiar to any historical era. It is a feature of a primitive mentality whether it is the mentality of the Bantu of Africa, of the primitive Indian of Guiana, or of the Jains who live today in India. The Jains believe that the "entire universe is filled with an infinite number . . . of individual souls" which may dwell in men, animals, plants, and even in "particles of earth, cold water, fire and wind."[15]

When one generalizes from anthropological data that the basic premise of all primitive life is animistic, he thereby formulates a theory about the underlying point of view of all primitive religions. This was the procedure of Edward Tylor, who in the last quarter of the last century developed the animistic theory,[16] which as Professor Wobbermin says, "dominated . . . the treatment . . . of primitive religion for a period of nearly four decades." At the end of the century, Wilhelm Wundt was responsible for further elaborating this hypothesis, with such success that Otto Pfleiderer maintained "animism is the practically undisputed basis upon which the still 'debatable questions concerning the beginnings of religion must be kept.' "[17]

According to the animistic theory, primitive men distinguish between bodies which move and the spirit in the body which accounts for its movement. This dualistic distinction, however, is clearer when stated as a hypothesis with which to interpret primitive religion than it probably is as the actual premise basic to primitive religion. Just how far back into human history this clear dualistic distinction, which is presupposed by animism, goes, is certainly problematic. It is, in fact, a distinction made by some primitive people today. Peasants of Lithuania, for example, think in terms of a spirit, or even a god, which causes the fermentation of beer. People living in the rural areas of South India believe in spirits, or deities, inhabiting every conceivable type of object. For them there is a water-goddess, a tiger-goddess, and a pearl-goddess called Challalamma who presides over the buttermilk.[18]

When it is believed that spirits dwell in objects, the significance of which is determined in part by the indwelling spirit, animism is both a type of philosophy and a type of religion. As a philosophy, it is an interpretation of the nature of objects whose movement is accounted for in terms of an indwelling spirit. As a religion, it is all that men do in taking these spirits into account for their supreme importance, because associated with objects which are of utmost significance to them. The catalogue of gods and goddesses for the primitive people of South India, would, therefore, be as inclusive as the realities which are significant in their lives. The very significance of a reality as essential in a primitive people's life is the basis for regarding it in a special way, and only those objects which are so significant, acquire a place in their religion.

When realities of special significance for men are interpreted, their significance is often accounted for in terms of a life-power or a spirit which inhabits them. It is this point of view that accounts for the interpretation of fetiches as spirit-inhabited. Whatever has utmost significance for primitive people is interpreted as a manifestation of a life-power, or life, a spirit, or soul. But as Sir James Frazer and R. R. Marett point out, the distinction between power, life-power, and individual spirits is not so clear for primitive men as it is for modern anthropologists. They therefore suggest a distinction between animism and animatism. Animism, as a primitive philosophy, is a belief that there is a spirit or a soul in things which move, whether these things are classified by civilized men as animate or as inanimate. As an anthropologist's theory, animism is a hypothesis about the philosophy and religion of primitive men. Animatism, on the other hand, is an anthropologist's category for classifying primitive philosophy as a belief that things which move are expressions of life, whether they are manifestations of an individual spirit, or of an indefinite life-power. Whether primitive men interpret all moving objects as alive, or as spirit-inhabited, is a debatable problem. But the distinction between the two concepts is at least clear in an anthropologist's vocabulary for interpreting primitive religions. Even though these ideas are perfectly clear as categories for classifying primitive beliefs, a perplexing problem nevertheless remains for every interpreter of primitive life: It is which data of primitive life should be put in which of these anthropological categories.

The categories for classifying thought are many. Their number is, of course, less for primitive thought than it is for the thought of civilized men, because the distinctions of which primitive men are aware are fewer than the distinctions of which civilized men are aware. But when distinctions made by primitive men are similar to distinctions made by civilized men, the same categories may be used for classifying similar distinctions. Elementary distinctions basic to primitive thought are premises for primitive philosophy and primitive religion, and when these same elementary distinctions are retained in civilized life, they are the bases for civilized philosophy and civilized religion. The primitive Zuñi, for example, believes that the entire world is animate. The early Ionian philosophers also believed that "soul is diffused through the whole universe."[19] The Zuñi believes that "all matter is alive," and a belief credited to the first of Ionian philosophers, Thales, is that "all things are full of gods."

A category for classifying this point of view in Ionian philosophy is "hylozoism," a term derived from the Greek words for matter and life. There is no reason, therefore, why this same category should not also be used to classify the thought of primitive men who have the same belief about the animate nature of the physical world as is credited to Thales. The Zuñis speak of the "earth mother (who) is replete with living waters," and for them, the "earth mother" is a symbol with which is associated the same sense as is associated with the term "gods" in Thales' philosophy. Both terms designate some reality which is other than a physical reality, whether it be water or the earth itself. Even the term "living waters" is not the same as the term "water." The distinction between a reality which animates water, and the water which is animated, is basic to primitive animatism, just as it is basic to the hylozoism of the early philosopher of Ionia, whose rudimentary speculation initiated the brilliant chapter in human history which all know as Greek philosophy.

There is also no fundamental difference between a philosophy of animism, which is basic to the religion of many primitive people, and a polytheistic mythology which is basic to the religion of many civilized people. The difference is primarily one of symbols. Basic to a polytheistic mythology is a personification of individual spirits, which according to the animistic point of view, are the ultimate causes for the movements of physical objects. The personification, for example, of the spirit or life which is believed to control the physical moon is called the goddess of the moon. The personification of the spirit or life believed to be in control of the movements of the physical sun is called the sun god. Thus the pantheons of ancient civilizations are the polytheistic counterparts of the animism or animatism of primitive people. The step from animism to polytheism is simply a stage in symbolism in which the individual soul, or life, identified with a particular object is personified, and is designated by a symbol whose features are derived from the features of human or even animal life.

In a polytheism there is no one ultimate reality. The pantheons of polytheistic religions are acknowledgments that there are many realities transcendent of human life and the physical world. Thus the belief in one reality, supreme over all other realities, is not essential to religious faith. It is only essential to the faith of some religions. But what is essential to some religions, such as the monotheistic faith of Islam, and what is essential to all religions, are two very different things. The faith of Islam is that there is one ultimate reality to which every other reality is subordinate. But for the religious life of many peoples, there is no comparable concept of complete subordination of all realities to one reality which is supreme in significance, because alone ultimate in existence. This distinction is not made in some civilized cultures, and it is safe to assert that it definitely is not an achievement of primitive mentality.

If religion is to be regarded as a universal phenomenon of human life, occurring in one form or another in all human cultures, irrespective of development, it obviously cannot be defined in terms of features which are peculiar to particular cultural developments. One feature, however, which is peculiar to cultural development, is symbolic. Without the benefit of mathematical symbols, for example, there could be no modern science of engineering. Yet even without mathematical symbols, primitive men did construct bridges, and did build boats and huts, by employing principles of engineering which were not symbolically expressed. A science of engineering would be impossible without mathematical symbols, or their equivalent, but a history of engineering, as a record of man's efforts to construct equipment to implement his life, would extend far behind the development of mathematics and the use of mathematical symbols.

A history of monotheistic religion would likewise extend no further back into human history than the concept of one reality supreme above all other realities, both in its ultimate status in existence and in its significance for human life. The history of religions, however, is not limited to the comparatively short history of monotheistic belief. Among the primitive Melanesians, there is no "notion of a Supreme Being," although there is "a belief in a force altogether distinct from the physical power which acts in all kinds of ways for good and evil."[20] This belief of the Melanesians is included in the category of religion because it is an acknowledgment of the relation of human life to a reality transcendent of human life and of human possessions, which is of supreme significance in human life. But if a belief in one supreme reality were essential to all religious life, no aspect of the primitive Melanesians' life could be included in the category of religious faith. Such an exclusion would be arbitrary, since it would make a particular symbolic expression of an interpretation more primary than the interpretation itself which is symbolically expressed.

The belief that there is one reality which alone is ultimate presupposes the capacity to conceive a unity above all multiplicity, and this capacity is basically an intellectual achievement. This intellectual achievement is a prerequisite for the spiritual life of a people affirming a thoroughgoing monotheistic or monistic faith. But such an achievement is not essential for the most rudimentary religious faith. The most rudimentary religious faith is not dependent upon particular intellectual achievements or a particular symbolism, and therefore should not be identified with anything peculiar to the history of philosophy or symbolism.

4. *Religious faith is a trust in a reality regarded as ultimate and revered for its supreme dependability in human life*

Religious faith is a trust in a reality regarded as dependable. Its dependability, according to religious faith, is its nature, which is no way dependent upon human life. An acknowledgment, however, of its significance for human life depends upon human life. An acknowledgment that there is a reality of supreme significance for human life, which is other than human life and the physical world, is, according to Aristotle, "an inspired utterance," because it contributes to human enlightenment. Man is enlightened when he understands the nature of the realities in relation to which he lives, and when he is aware of his relation to a reality which does not depend either upon himself or the physical world, but is worthy to be trusted for its ultimate dependability; religious life is one condition for his enlightenment. It was because Aristotle believed that there is a reality other than the physical world upon which the physical world depends for an essential feature of its nature that he regarded the religious tradition preserving "the ancient treasure" of this "inspired utterance" as a mark of human wisdom.

Aristotle was aware of the differences between his philosophy in its developed form and the beliefs of "forefathers in the most remote ages ... handed down to their posterity."[21] But he was also aware of the similarity of the ancient belief underlying religious life and the basic premise underlying his own metaphysic. His metaphysic is an expression of extraordinary intelligence, yet the basic premise of his metaphysic is not unique to his intelligence, any more than it is unique to the tradition of Greek philosophy. The basic premise of his metaphysic shares with all religious life the "inspired utterance" that there is a reality transcendent of the physical world upon which the physical world depends, whose significance for human life is not a feature of the physical world.

It would be incautious to stipulate a particular metaphysic as essential for religious life, since many interpretations of the nature of reality are compatible with religious faith. But any metaphysic which is compatible with religious faith rests upon the basic premise that there is a reality other than human life and other than the physical world. The first premise of religious faith is that there is a reality which is not subject to the fluctuations of the physical order, any more than it is subject to the caprice of human loyalties and human affections. As transcendent of human life and the physical world, its status depends upon neither, yet both depend ultimately upon it for what is essential to their natures.

The belief that there is a reality which is essential to the physical world and to human life, which is other than both, is basic to Aristotle's metaphysic as well as to all religious life. Aristotle, however, did not formulate his metaphysic primarily for its religious significance. Its primary significance for him was intellectual. It is an expression of his desire to reduce to systematic order his interpretations of the nature of the physical world. Since he believed that the ultimate source of motion in the physical world is other than the physical world itself, he believed that the status of its ultimate mover is essential to the nature of the physical world. The Unmoved Mover of the physical world is the supremely significant reality in Aristotle's cosmology, since he believed that without its role as the source of movement, there would be no eternal motion of the heavenly bodies. The metaphysic of Democritus, on the other hand, rests upon the premise that the motion in the physical world is intrinsic to physical bodies. Thus the radical difference between the metaphysic of Democritus and the metaphysic of Aristotle consists in the basic premise about the source of motion in the physical world. A moving body in the physical world is, according to Aristotle, a sign of a reality transcendent of the physical world. According to Democritus, on the other hand, a moving body in the physical world refers to nothing transcendent of the physical world. Its nature is a function of its relations to other physical bodies within the physical world. Democritus specifically denies any reference of a physical body beyond the physical world, since for him the physical world is itself the ultimate reality, and it is this premise of his metaphysic which repudiates religious faith. For religious faith, the physical world is not ultimate, but is a sign of another reality which is ultimate.

The particular signs which perform symbolic functions are peculiar to cultures, and are conditioned by intelligence. The pictorial image of "Child of the Water," for example, is peculiar to the mentality of the primitive Apache capable only of comprehending concrete signs rather than abstract symbols. Yet, insofar as the figure "Child of the Water" refers to a reality other than the earth, which is revered because the earth is believed ultimately to depend upon it, the figure is religiously significant, and its role in religious life is due to its referential function. This referential function is not a peculiarity of any specific sign, but is a function of any object which refers beyond itself to another reality. This function, therefore, is performed as effectively for the Apache by the pictorial image "Child of the Water" as it is performed for Aristotle by the symbol "Unmoved Mover."

The mentality of the Apache is not the mentality of Aristotle, and neither is his symbolic equipment equivalent to Aristotle's. But insofar as both use symbols to designate a reality other than the physical order with which each is acquainted, and which each acknowledges to be of ultimate significance, both share in common one aspect of mentality. It is the capacity to think in terms of signs which refer to a reality of supreme importance.

If points of view comparable to the metaphysic of Aristotle and the cosmogony of the Apaches are to be brought under one category of religious life, it is obvious that peculiarities of signs cannot be essential to religious life. It is also apparent that certain details of metaphysics cannot be essential to religious life. The Apache, for example, believes that the earth was created. Aristotle does not believe this. According to him the entire physical world is uncreated, and as such is eternal. But the premise which is common to Aristotle's metaphysic and to the creation story of the Apache is that there is a reality transcendent of the physical order. This is the one feature of a metaphysic which is essential to religious life. It is a belief that there is a reality more ultimate than the physical order itself, upon which the physical world and human life are finally dependent, and which is therefore worthy of man's supreme reverence.

Chapter Four

THE SYMBOLS OF RELIGIOUS METAPHYSICS

1. *The symbols of religious faith refer to a reality transcendent of human life and the physical world*

A belief which is basic to religious faith is that a reality exists transcendent of human life and the physical world, which is supremely worthy of man's trust and reverence. This belief is the primary premise affirmed in one form or another in every religion, irrespective of its cultural background. The Sumerians, for example, who were among the most ancient of civilized peoples, did not regard even the sun as ultimate, but believed that it was derived from the air.[1] The non-determinate character of air probably impressed them as antecedent to any more determinate reality. Yet, the symbol with which they referred to the reality from which the sun was believed to have originated is the same symbol with which they referred to the air they breathe.

If there is one obvious principle in symbolism, it is that symbols which are physically identical do not always have the same sense. The symbol by means of which the Sumerians referred to the air men breathe does not have the same sense as the symbol for the reality from which heavenly bodies have their origin. Because the particular symbol selected by the Sumerians has a connotation of a substance as common as the air men breathe, it should not, therefore, be inferred that the air men breathe is the reality they regarded as ultimate in the order of existence. The process by which the ancient Sumerians arrived at the symbol "air" for the ultimate reality is probably the same as that of Anaximenes, the Ionian philosopher, who also referred to the ultimate reality as air. If, therefore, one should regard the cosmology of the Sumerians as naive, he would be inconsistent not to regard the metaphysic of Anaximenes as equally naive. And yet, the influence of Anaximenes in the history of Greek philosophy has been considerable.

One would likewise be guilty of the most arbitrary of procedures if he were to classify the explanation of the ancient Sumerians as mythology, and the explanation of Anaximenes as philosophy. A radical distinction may not be made between the mythologies and the philosophies of ancient civilizations any more than a radical distinction may be made between their cosmologies and their cosmogonies. Every attempt of men to interpret the nature of the world in which they live is motivated by the same fundamental desire to understand. It is purely an accident of symbolism that some men state their interpretations in the pictorial figures of a myth. When the function of a myth is to articulate an interpretation, there is no fundamental difference between a myth and a philosophy. The difference is primarily a matter of symbolism.

Interpretations which have been stated in pictorial language have, however, traditionally been classified as mythology. But when one penetrates beyond the superficial features of symbols to the motives underlying their use, he is less impressed by the difference of symbols, and is more impressed by the identity of human motivation in their use.

Religious life is a striving to understand the nature of an ultimate reality, and when in the process of this striving, one reality refers men to another reality, it performs for them the role of a sign. A language sign which the ancient Hindus used to designate a "god of the sky" was Varuna. But as a god of the sky, Varuna was not the ultimate reality. He was the ultimate reality only when interpreted as "the all-embracing Heavens."[2] Thus when the symbol "Varuna" refers to "the all-embracing Heavens" its religious significance is not the same as when it designates only "a sky god." In one use, the symbol designates the ultimate reality. In the other use, it designates a reality which is subordinate to a more ultimate reality.

The specific significance which a symbol performs in religious life is therefore not a feature of the symbol as a physical sign. It is a feature of the sense of the symbol, and this is determined by its specific role in religious life. When, for example, the sense of the symbol "Brahman" is "that from whence these beings are born, that by which, when born, they live, that into which they enter at their death . . . that on which the worlds are founded and their inhabitants,"[3] the symbol "Brahman" refers unmistakably to the reality in quest of which all religious life earnestly strives. What is unfamiliar, however, to religious individuals who are not acquainted with the tradition of Hindu faith is the symbol "Brahman" or "Brahma" for designating the ultimate reality. But every religious life, within the limits set by the culture to which it is indigenous, believes as does the Hindu, for whom there is an ultimate reality "on which the worlds are founded and their inhabitants."

The religious Hindu desires above all things to return to this reality from which he believes he ultimately is derived, and so he desires to forego every aspect of life which he believes separates him from it. One must ask himself, therefore, how this desire of the devout Hindu differs from the desire of Plotinus, and from all Christian mystics who have been influenced by his philosophy. One may ask specifically how it differs from the Christian mystic Tersteegen, who, referring to God, declares, "I in thee, Thou in me, let me vanish wholly to see and find Thee only." The mysticism of Tersteegen may in turn cite a Scriptural basis in St. Paul's affirmation that "the Lord is that Spirit," which Professor Seeberg interprets to mean "the spiritual Energy which forms the world and shapes history."[4]

If the accidents of symbolism did not so successfully separate men from each other, the vine and the branches of which Jesus speaks would not be so difficult a parable to understand. If a religious individual who was not born into an oriental culture were to understand the teachings of Buddha, for example, rather than be distressed by his unfamiliar symbols, he would recognize that religious faith is not dependent upon any particular language. Buddha taught that "there is a not-born, a not-created, a not-formed," a knowledge of which is the essential condition for enlightened life in the world "which is come to pass, the created, the formed."[5] When one understands his teachings, and is not primarily impressed with the peculiarity of his language, he understands that there is a common conviction underlying religious life, notwithstanding the vast amount of all that has arisen in the course of human history to conceal the basic unity of religious faith.

Religious life as a human phenomenon comprehends the particular faith of many peoples. Thus religious life has common basic beliefs, even though it is not expressed in the same symbolic forms. But wherever it occurs, it struggles within the limits of its culture to understand the nature of the ultimate reality to which it seeks to give reverence.

For the ancient Chinese of the Shang period, fifteen hundred years or more B.C., the symbol for the ultimate reality was "Shang-ti." When the Shang civilization was subsequently incorporated into the succeeding civilization of the Chou period, the symbol "Shang-ti" was partially displaced by the symbol "T'ien." The sense of the symbol "Shang-ti" as "Lord of Heaven" referred to a reality more ultimate than the physical world and human life. The sense of the symbol "T'ien" as "a Supreme Power and a Supreme Ruler"[6] also referred to an ultimate reality upon which the physical world and all people were believed to be dependent. Many changes occurred in the fusion of these ancient civilizations. Even the symbols by which their religious faith was expressed underwent change. But underlying the changes was the same fundamental faith.

Language symbols may be as different as the grammars of language are different, yet they may have an identical sense when used to express a belief which is not peculiar to any one culture, or any one era. The Chinese people, for example, had a religious faith before the time of Confucius, and it was into a culture with a religious faith that Confucius himself was born. It is, therefore, understandable why he not only inherited the language of his culture, but also the sense of his vocabulary. The teachings of Confucius are primarily moral, since they emphasize man's responsibilities to his state and to his family. But they also acknowledge man's responsibilities to T'ien or Heaven, and it is this acknowledgment which is the religious element in his teachings.

The religious significance of his teachings depends upon the acknowledgment of the ultimate dependence of human life upon a reality transcendent of the physical world. Whether "T'ien" designates "the Lord of Heaven," or "Heaven" makes no fundamental difference, provided either connotation of the symbol denotes the ultimate reality. When, however, the symbol "T'ien" is used specifically to denote the physical heavens, as it is by Hsün Tzu, one of the disciples of Confucius, it does not have the same religious significance as it has when it refers beyond the physical heavens. According to Hsün Tzu, "Heaven has a constant regularity of action . . . The fixed stars make their round; the sun and moon alternately shine; the four seasons come in succession."

When the regularity of the physical heavens is the aspect of reality to which exclusive attention is given, such attention is more defensibly classified as "aesthetic" then as "religious." Just where an aesthetic experience ends and a religious experience begins is a matter for dispute, a resolution of which must finally rest upon a definition of both religious experience and aesthetic experience. When, however, man's awe for the beauty of the ordered heavens moves him to reflect upon the source of its order, and moves him to acknowledge with reverence that there is a reality even more ultimate than the heavenly bodies, his awe may well be classified as a religious experience. It is a religious experience because of the function of the heavens for referring his attention to another reality which he regards as more ultimate, and so esteems as more worthy of his supreme reverence.

Lao-tzu was born into the same culture as Confucius, and he too was destined to become a founder of one of the great bodies of religious faith. Lao-tzu and Confucius, however, differed in their vocabularies, and in the sense of the terms in their vocabularies. The particular term which Lao-tzu selected for expressing his religious faith is "Tao," and it is for this reason that he is referred to as the founder of Taoism.

As a religion, Taoism is the faith that there is a Way, or Tao, by which all men may find dependable guidance in life and by means of which they may acquire an enlightenment that will save them from the needless suffering of unenlightened life. This Way "existed before heaven and earth . . . dependent on nothing, unchanging, all pervading, unfailing."[7]

This basic belief of Lao-tzu is thus a faith about an ultimate reality, which is "the path of that which is so-of-itself." It is "the Self-existent Being." This faith of Lao-tzu is religious because Tao is believed to be both the "Way of man"—the means for attaining a completely trustworthy guidance in human life, and also the "Way of the universe"—the ultimate principle of order in the physical world.

Whether this ultimate factor of order in the universe and in man's life is referred to as "Shang-ti," as "T'ien," or as "Tao," is not religiously significant. What is religiously significant is that throughout the history of China there has been a religious faith whose prophets have been many. But many though the prophets have been, there has been one reality to which they have testified. All have affirmed the faith that there is one reality, ultimate in existence, and so supreme in significance for human life. Acknowledged as other than man's possessions, it is also acknowledged as other than man's symbols.

That it is other than all of man's symbols is itself a religious faith. It is a faith that what is utmost in significance for human life, and so worthy above every other reality to be worshiped, is not dependent for its existence upon the accidents of man's culture. The conviction of the dependability of an ultimate reality, which in no way is dependent for its nature upon man's resources, has persisted throughout the history of the religious life of the Chinese. This fact accounts for the success with which both the Mohammedan and the Christian missionaries to China established considerable followings. It accounts in no negligible measure for the effectiveness of the Nestorian missionaries, who, entering China in the eighth century, believed that all who "wander long from the *Way*" will live in "deepened darkness."[8] It accounts also for the prayer made by the Emperor of China on the Altar of Heaven:[9]

"O thou great God . . .
All that lives is beholden to Thee for Thy goodness. . . .
Thou alone are the fount of all things."

The sign-function of the physical world as the basis for its religious significance is likewise clearly expressed by the Zoroastrian who asks, "What artist made light and darkness: Who made morning, noon, and night?"[10] The belief that there is an ultimate reality transcendent of the physical bodies of the heavens is a religious faith, and also a premise basic to a particular type of metaphysic. There is, therefore, no fundamental difference between a metaphysic and a religious faith in the knowledge-claims about such an ultimate reality. There is, however, a fundamental difference in the roles which such knowledge-claims assume in an individual's life. Any knowledge-claim about the nature of an ultimate reality is a metaphysical judgment. When this belief about an ultimate reality specifically motivates an individual to revere the ultimate reality for its supreme importance in his life, it is a religious faith. Whether a belief about the nature of an ultimate reality is classified as a metaphysical premise, or as a religious faith, is of no fundamental significance. It is a matter of naming, and the particular name which is assigned is arbitrary. What is not arbitrary, however, is the role which such a belief performs in an individual's life.

The difference between the role of a metaphysical belief about an ultimate reality and the role of a religious faith is the difference between a philosophy about ultimate reality and a religious life which acknowledges that man is dependent upon the ultimate reality for all that he cherishes in his life. The Zoroastrian belief, for example, that the heavenly bodies are ultimately dependent upon a reality from which they derive their nature is also basic to the Zoroastrian religious affirmation, "I strive to recognize by these things, Thee, O Mazda, Creator of all things."

The belief that there is a reality more ultimate than the physical world is a premise basic to all religious faith, and it is also a premise basic to some philosophies of the nature of the physical world. The difference, therefore, between the religious significance of a belief and its philosophical significance is not the assumed knowledge-character of the belief. It is rather the role which the belief performs in an individual's life.

This distinction is clear in the pre-Socratic philosophers of

Greece, who, regardless of their traditional classification as naturalists, believed there is a first principle in terms of which they proposed to account for the creation, emanation, or differentiation of every reality other than the first principle. The history of early Greek philosophy is therefore primarily a record of belief about the nature of such an ultimate reality—about its role in the physical world and in human life. For Thales, "this first principle . . . is water," "getting the idea," as Aristotle suggests, from the fact that "the nourishment of all things is moist," and also from the fact that "the germs of all beings are of a moist nature."[11] For his "pupil and successor," Anaximander, "the first principle is one . . . and infinite." Simplicius points out that when Anaximander observed the "four elements changing into one another he (did) not deem it right to make any one of these the underlying substance," or "the first principle," which is "eternal and does not grow old." It "surrounds all the worlds" which come "into being and pass away."[12] The distinction, therefore, which Anaximander makes between physical worlds, which come into being and pass away, and a reality which as ultimate "is eternal and does not grow old," is the same distinction which underlies the metaphysic of religious faith.

2. *The intended role of a symbol which designates the ultimate reality differentiates philosophical speculation and religious faith*

There is a fundamental difference between a philosophy of ultimate reality and a religious faith. Religious faith expresses itself as a reverent adjustment to the reality which man regards as ultimate, and which he esteems for its supreme significance because he believes that he is ultimately dependent upon it for everything in his life which he cherishes. A philosophy of ultimate reality, on the other hand, is an interpretation whose motivation is primarily to understand the nature of the total context in which man lives.

The ultimate reality for the Milesian philosophers, whether called water, Boundless (*Apeiron*), or air, was an explanatory principle, and the motive for their interpretations of the ultimate reality was speculative. They wanted to understand. The primary purpose in religious life, however, for understanding the nature of the ultimate reality is that man may know better how to give his utmost reverence to it as first in the order of existence.

A designation of ultimate reality by the term "god" is not alone determinative of the distinction between a metaphysic which is religiously significant and one which is not. It is not indicative of a metaphysic of religious significance in early Greek philosophy, for example, since in maintaining that "all things are full of gods"[13] Thales meant only that the gods worshiped by his contemporaries were not ultimate, but were explicable in terms of a reality more ultimate than their individual natures. He thus distinguished an ultimate reality from realities which are not ultimate, and since, according to him, the gods of Greek polytheism are not ultimate, they should not be regarded as if they were.

If, however, after making this distinction between what is ultimate and what is not ultimate, Thales had done all that he believed was worthy of him to do in revering the Ultimate, there would be no fundamental warrant for denying the religious significance of his metaphysic, even though he denies the ultimate nature of the gods.

What is important in a philosophy of religion, however, is not a classification of individuals as religious or otherwise. The warning of the Scriptures in this regard must be respected. Distinguishing between who is religious and who is not is a presumption that is not one of man's rights. What is important, however, in a philosophy of religion is a distinction between a metaphysic which is a factor in religious life, and a metaphysic which is not. This distinction does not depend upon the extent of an individual's knowledge of an ultimate reality, but rather on what he does with his assumed knowledge of an ultimate reality.

A reality is religiously significant only when an acknowledgment of its nature as ultimate motivates a reverence for it as supreme in significance above every other reality. When the existence of a god is acknowledged, but its nature is not believed to be ultimate in the order of reality, its significance for human life is not supreme over every other reality. "Infinite air is the first principle," according to Anaximenes, and "gods and divine beings" are derived from air. This assumed derivation of gods from a reality more ultimate than themselves specifically implies that for Anaximenes gods are not ultimate in the order of reality. His distinction between gods and an ultimate reality is, however, not irreverent. It is rather an expression of his repudiation of the popular polytheism of his contemporaries.

Since polytheism is incompatible with the basic premise of a philosophical monism, Anaximenes depreciated popular polytheism as a failure to understand that there is one ultimate reality. According to a polytheism, there are many realities, all of which may be equally ultimate in the sense that no one of them is necessarily dependent for its nature upon another. Although the mythology underlying a polytheistic religion often is a dramatic account of the derivation of one god from another, or of the creation of one god by another, the order of existence was never treated in Greek polytheism as a fundamental problem. When, however, it was recognized as a fundamental problem, Milesian philosophy arose in distinction to Greek polytheism, as a criticism of its intellectual unsatisfactoriness, and so of its religious inadequacy.

An interpretation of the nature of reality which is not intellectually satisfying to an individual who earnestly endeavors as best he can to understand the nature of the world in which he lives cannot enter into his religious life. A religious individual takes advantage of every source of enlightenment available to him in his attempt to understand the nature of the world in which he lives, even though he does not seek such enlightenment primarily for speculation, but rather for worship.

A religious individual directs his worship to the reality he esteems as supremely worthy of his reverence, and a reality which he regards as ultimate is the only one which he esteems as worthy of his utmost reverence. The reality which is worthy of worship is, according to a religious individual, supreme above every other reality in the order of significance for human life because first in the order of existence. Although there is no evidence that the Milesian philosophers revered such an ultimate reality as alone worthy of their worship, their motive to differentiate it from what is not ultimate is compatible with the motivation of religious life.

One religious life may differ from another in enlightenment, but irrespective of what is known, the motive of all religious life is to give reverence to the reality which is supremely worthy of it, and this reality is, for religious life, the Ultimate.

3. *A symbol for acknowledging an ultimate reality must be distinguished from any particular interpretation of an ultimate reality*

The reality which is supremely significant in religious life is not a symbol. It is the reality to which some symbols refer. The reality which is ultimate, and so dependent for its nature upon nothing, is the only intended referent of a symbol of supreme religious significance. Every symbol is a human device, and every interpretation which constitutes the sense of a symbol is man's intellectual and spiritual achievement. What is not man's achievement, however, and so in no way depends upon what man believes, is the reality to which religious life is oriented. When this reality is designated by the term "God," the theistic symbol has a religious significance which no other symbol has. When, therefore, this symbol has been assigned the exclusive role of designating the ultimate reality, it is no longer an arbitrary symbol in religious life. It is the one symbol of supreme religious significance. But more than one term may be selected by various individuals to perform this unique symbolic role. Hence all terms are equally significant in religious life when they perform the symbolic function of designating the reality most worthy to receive man's homage.

Parmenides, the philosopher whom Plato regarded as "a man to be reverenced"[14] for his wisdom, revealed one aspect of his wisdom when he spoke about the symbols which men use to refer to the ultimate reality: "All these things," he declared, are "but a name."[15] The reality, however, which is of supreme significance in religious life is, as he declares, "without beginning," and, therefore, is not a name.

The particular name which man selects to designate the ultimate reality is arbitrary in the sense meant by Heraclitus when he pointed out that "everyone gives . . . the name he pleases."[16] But the sense of the term which interprets the reality that man endeavors to worship as supremely significant is not arbitrary. This reality, according to the interpretation of Heraclitus, "always was, and is, and ever shall be," and is "the intelligence by which all things are steered." This interpretation is the basic conviction of his metaphysic, since it is a statement of his understanding of the nature of the physical world and its relation to a reality upon which he believes it is ultimately dependent for its order. The particular name, however, by which he designates the ultimate source of its order is a peculiarity of the language he spoke. Realizing the arbitrary character of all language terms, he declared that the ultimate reality is "willing and it is unwilling to be called by the name Zeus."[17] What is philosophically significant, therefore, is not the particular name he used for designating the ultimate source of order in the physical world, although he did prefer the term "Logos" to the term "Zeus." What is philosophically significant is the sense of the term, since its sense is the interpretation which constitutes his metaphysic.

The sense of a symbol, rather than the symbol itself, is what is religiously significant. The ultimate reality may be worshiped with equal reverence when it is referred to as Elohim, Yahweh, Jehovah, God, Allah, or Zeus. The profound wisdom of Cleanthes is, therefore, expressed in his great *Hymn to Zeus* which begins: "O God most glorious, called by many a name, Nature's great king, through endless years the same." Irrespective of the specific symbols which men select, they are of equal significance when they designate the reality which is alone supremely worthy of reverence.

Religion cannot be defined in terms of reverence alone, but neither can it be defined without taking into account man's endeavor to revere the reality he regards as ultimate. Without such a motive there is no religious life, even though man may believe that there is an ultimate reality to which, in one way or another, all other realities are subordinate and upon which they are dependent.

Religious life must always include the belief that there is a reality whose significance for human life is supreme above all other realities. This qualification may be fulfilled by the Greek concept Fate (Moira or Destiny), as well as by other concepts. Insofar as Fate is interpreted as an ultimate determinant of an individual's life, and is esteemed for its supreme importance in his life, in relation to which he acknowledges his final dependence, even Fate may be religiously significant.

The criteria for ascertaining the religious significance of symbols are not peculiarities of symbols. They are features of an individual's faith. The individual who is reverent before a reality he esteems as supreme in significance for his life, because ultimate in the order of existence, is religious, not by virtue of his vocabulary, but by virtue of his faith.

The object of religious worship is a reality esteemed as ultimate and revered for its pre-eminent role in man's life. The particular symbol for designating it is of no fundamental consequence. An acknowledgment of it may be non-verbal, as the reverent "raising of the hands," or it may be verbal, as the reverent phrase in the Upanishads, "That art Thou" (*Tat twam asi*).[18] The motivation of human life to give homage to the reality it acknowledges as ultimate in existence is the only factor of consequence for distinguishing one belief about an ultimate reality as religiously significant from another belief about an ultimate reality which is not religiously significant.

The religious significance of a belief, therefore, is a feature of a life which believes that there is a reality supremely worthy to be revered, and does what it believes is appropriate for expressing its reverence. Parmenides, for example, acknowledges the supreme significance of the role of Fate, when he declares, "Nor is there nor will there be anything apart from being; for fate has linked it together."[19] The ultimate factor accounting for the ordered character of reality is also designated by the same term in some passages in the philosophy of Heraclitus, according to whom the "fixed cycles to all eternity" are "determined by destiny."[20] It is, however, of no fundamental consequence in the metaphysic of Heraclitus whether the symbol "fate" or "destiny" or "logos" is selected to designate this ultimate reality. What is of consequence in his metaphysic is the connotation of the terms "fate," "destiny," and "logos," since all these terms have equivalent symbolic significance insofar as they designate the ultimate explanatory factor for the ordered character of the multiple phenomena of the physical world.

4. *The particular symbol selected to designate an ultimate reality is not of primary importance either in a speculative philosophy or in a religious life*

The essential aspect of a symbol is not its physical characteristics, but its function in referring to a reality, an interpretation of which is its sense. Thus what is of primary importance in an interpretation of the nature of ultimate reality is not the particular symbol selected to constitute a shorthand means for indicating the interpretation. The interpretation itself is the significant factor both in a speculative philosophy and in a religious life.

That the symbol as such is of no primary consequence becomes apparent when one analyzes, for example, the sense of the symbol "Zeus," which Aeschylus uses in preference to the symbol "Fate" used by Homer. After distinguishing between the symbols "Zeus" and "Fate," Aeschylus, however, uses the symbol "Zeus" as Homer uses the symbol "Fate," which means that he designates the ultimate reality believed to be responsible for both good and evil by the symbol "Zeus." The distinction between symbols as such in the metaphysics of Homer and Aeschylus is, therefore, not itself of critical significance. This fact is made clear by Plato, who, also using the symbols "Zeus" or "God" as Aeschylus does, nevertheless does not use them with the same sense as does Aeschylus. Plato specifically repudiates the belief maintained by Aeschylus that "God can be the author of evil." The fundamental difference in their beliefs is thus not dependent upon symbols. It is dependent rather upon their interpretations of the ultimate reality which constitute the senses of the symbols they use.

A fundamental motivation underlying one of the great traditions in Greek philosophy is an attempt to interpret the nature of an ultimate reality believed to be responsible for the ordered character of the physical world. The first school of Greek philosophy to undertake this task was founded by Pythagoras, who believed that numbers are "the first principles of all things."[21] Thus the concept of "numbers" performs for Pythagoras a role which the concept of "Fate" performed for Homer, and the concept of "Zeus" performed for Aeschylus. Each one of these three Greek thinkers endeavored in his own way to interpret the nature of an ultimate reality believed to be of utmost significance in the physical world, and also of significance in human life.

The symbol which Anaxagoras used to designate the ultimate source of order is Mind (*Nous*). He declares that "Whatever things shall be, all these Mind arranged in order; and it arranged that rotation, according to which now rotate stars and sun and moon and air and aether."[22] Thus the terms are many by which the ultimate reality has been designated in Greek philosophy. Yet, a fundamental similarity persists throughout Greek metaphysical philosophy insofar as an ultimate reality is believed to be the explanatory factor for an essential feature of the physical world.

The essential feature of the physical world with which some Greek philosophers were primarily concerned is the ordered nature of its phenomena. The essential feature with which others were primarily concerned is the source of its motion. No Greek philosopher before Plato, however, was perplexed about the actual origin of the physical world, and it is specifically to this problem that Plato directed himself in one of the last of his writings. He alone of the early Greek philosophers maintains the belief affirmed in *Genesis* that "God created the heaven and the earth." For the writer of *Genesis*, however, it was the earth which was "without form," whereas for Plato it was the Receptacle which was without form until operated upon by the ordering activity of God. One aspect of Plato's metaphysic as stated in the *Timaeus* is not, therefore, essentially different from one aspect of the metaphysic which underlies the first chapter of *Genesis*. What is obviously different is the philosophical vocabulary of Plato which he inherited from the culture in which he lived, just as the writer of *Genesis* inherited his vocabulary from the culture in which he lived. Regardless of the differences in their vocabularies, there is a fundamental similarity in their basic convictions.

Whether an interpretation of the nature of an ultimate reality is expressed in the vocabulary of "Logos," "Mind," or "God," the particular symbol is not of primary significance. What is of primary significance is the interpretation which constitutes its sense. Insofar as "Mind" designates for Anaxagoras the ultimate reality which "ruled the rotation of the whole," and which "arranged that rotation, according to which now rotate stars and sun and moon and air," the symbolic role of Mind is identical with the symbolic role of "the Spirit of God (which) moved upon the face of the waters"; which "divided the light from darkness."

One motive of philosophers is to understand the nature of ultimate reality. This is also a motive of religious life. But the motive of religious life in endeavoring to understand the nature of ultimate reality is that man may revere it. Religious life is the earnest orientation of human life to the ultimate reality in order that man may direct to it the homage he believes is its due because of its pre-eminent role in existence. Without this specific endeavor to understand the nature of ultimate reality, there would be no philosophical tradition of metaphysics; and without the endeavor to revere the reality which is believed to be ultimate, there would be no religious life.

Individuals, however, who do not interpret the vast extent of reality as ultimately subordinate to one reality, do not believe that there is only one reality which is of supreme speculative significance. They may, nevertheless, be religious insofar as they believe that what is ultimate ought to be revered with the most respectful homage of which men are capable, whether it is one or more than one. Religious life is not a function of any particular metaphysic, even though there is no religious life without some metaphysic.

The metaphysic which is basic to religious life is monistic when it is believed that there is one reality prior to all other realities in the order of existence, and so in the order of significance for human life. With a monistic metaphysic, religious life may be monotheistic, or it may even be something other than monotheistic. It is, however, specifically monotheistic when it affirms the belief that "in the beginning," one ultimate reality "created the heaven and the earth." When, on the other hand, it is believed that there is an ultimate reality other than God, for whose existence God is not responsible, man may affirm a monotheistic religious faith even though he does not maintain a monistic metaphysic.

Monotheistic religious faith should not, therefore, be carelessly identified with a monistic metaphysic. One may believe that there is one ultimate reality and be a monotheist in his religious faith; but he may also be unable to believe that the God whom he worships as trustworthy above every other reality is also responsible for every form of existence. In this case, his monotheistic faith is not an adaptation to his non-monistic metaphysic.

Essential to every metaphysic basic to religious life is a belief that there is a reality supremely worthy to be revered for its pre-eminent significance in human life. The criterion of the religious significance of an ultimate reality is its worthiness to be revered above every other reality. For some philosophers, however, such as Chu Hsi, the ultimate reality, which he calls "tai-chi," is undifferentiated, and as such it cannot be revered in any form of worship, since the referent of worship is always distinguished from other realities which are not equally revered. A metaphysic which postulates an ultimate reality which is undifferentiated, such as "tai-chi" in the philosophy of Chu Hsi, or the One in the philosophy of Plotinus, or the Absolute for metaphysical idealisms, repudiates religious worship, and does so for a purely logical reason.[23]

Chu Hsi maintains that the first differentiation of "tai-chi" is two principles: one the principle of light, and the other the principle of darkness. He specifically identifies the principle of light, *Yang*, with *T'ien*, or Heaven. When, therefore, this identification is made, Heaven is not regarded as the ultimate reality, but is interpreted as derived from a reality more ultimate than it. Thus the reality designated by the symbol "T'ien" is not of supreme religious significance for Chu Hsi, since in his metaphysic it is not regarded as an ultimate reality.

What is of primary significance in a monistic metaphysic is the intellectual motivation to press the mind to a point where it conceives one reality more ultimate than all other realities. This, however, is not only the motive of every monistic metaphysic, but also that of every religious faith which affirms the belief that even though there are many eternal realities, there is one reality of supreme significance, which above all others is worthy of man's homage.

Some metaphysic is essential to religious faith, although no one particular metaphysic is essential to it. What alone is essential to religious life is the earnest desire to give homage to the reality believed to be supremely worthy of man's reverence. When it is believed that more than one reality is worthy of reverence, because ultimately determinative either of an aspect of the world or of an essential aspect of his life, then some form of pluralistic metaphysic is maintained. When these several realities are referred to as gods, some type of polytheism is a feature of some religious life. The primitive Hopi and Zuñi Indians, for example, believe "in the existence of a large group of supernatural beings, the *kachinas*."[24] The ancient Sumerians believed that there are many "superhuman and immortal beings" which they designated by the term *dingir*, translated "god."[25]

When the Sumerians, however, were defeated by the Babylonian empire, they inferred that their gods were likewise superseded in power by the gods of the Babylonians. The Canaanites also identified the power of their empire with the pre-eminent significance of their gods, and when their empire suffered, they too concluded that there are other realities more ultimate than their gods. Thus failing to believe that there is one reality supreme above every other reality, both in the order of existence and also in the order of significance for human life, primitive and civilized people alike direct their worship to many gods.

Their failure to comprehend one reality supreme above all others is fundamentally an intellectual failure, which in turn is basic to their religious failure to revere one reality supreme in significance above all other realities. In consequence of their failure to comprehend one ultimate reality upon which every other reality depends, they direct their homage to a multiplicity of realities, each of which is assumed under some particular circumstance to be of utmost significance. When, however, human life is not oriented to a reality which actually is ultimate, it is subject to the disillusionment inevitable to all deficient knowledge. Such disillusionment is inevitable even in religious life when the reality which is trusted and revered as ultimate is not an ultimate reality. Man's failure to know the reality which actually is supremely worthy of his trust, and so of his worship, is a handicap to his religious life. But even with such a deficiency in knowledge, man may still be religious by virtue of his earnest striving to know the nature of the reality most worthy to be trusted.

5. *Man's endeavor to express his religious faith may give rise to intellectual perplexities*

The belief that there is a reality transcendent of human life and the physical world is a universal feature of religious faith. This belief is not, however, unique to religious life. What specifically is unique to religious life is the belief that this reality is supremely worthy to be trusted.

A reality which in any way depends either upon man's life or the physical world is subject to change. This interpretation of the changing nature of the physical world, which is basic to religious faith, is also basic to the philosophies of Heraclitus and Plato. Both Heraclitus and Plato believe that if there were no reality other than the changing world, there would be no possibility for trustworthy knowledge. Knowledge, in distinction to opinion, according to them, is not subject to change, and hence an object of unchanging knowledge must likewise be unchanging. Both, therefore, assume that the only warrant for claiming a knowledge which is not subject to incessant revision is the existence of a reality which is not subject to change, and so is other than human life and other than the physical world. The term by which Heraclitus refers to this reality is "Logos." The term by which Plato refers to it is "the Idea of the Good."

If a religious individual in a primitive culture were to formulate the most general conviction basic to his religious faith, it would not be unlike the premise which is basic to the metaphysics of Heraclitus and Plato, since the belief that there is a reality transcendent of human life and the physical world is logically prior to any particular interpretation of its nature.

Although it would be indefensible to press primitive religious life into the categories of advanced Greek philosophy, it would be no less indefensible to ignore a belief which is basic to primitive religious life and logically prior to any particular philosophical expansion. A belief, however, which is not unique to any particular religious or philosophical development is that there is a reality transcendent of human life and the physical world, which in no way is dependent for its status either upon human life or upon the physical world. This belief is basic to religious life even though it is not developed into a theology. As a belief about the nature of an ultimate reality, it is a metaphysic, even though it is not expanded into a metaphysical system.

The metaphysical premise which is basic to religious life is not necessarily a belief that the ultimate reality is God. If the theistic belief were essential to religious life, primitive dynamism, animatism, and animism could not be classified as types of religion, and neither could polytheisms be included in the category of religion. Any particular interpretation of a reality believed to be transcendent of human life and the physical world is, therefore, secondary to the belief that there is such a reality. The belief that there is such a reality of supreme significance for human life is the one metaphysical premise essential to religious life, and is therefore affirmed in one way or another in all religions. A theistic belief is one type of human interpretation of a reality believed to be transcendent of human life and the physical world. But as a particular type of metaphysic, it is not a criterion of religious belief, although it may be a criterion of the truth of religious belief.

Believing that there is a reality of pre-eminent significance for human life, which is transcendent of human life and the physical world, religious individuals enlist all of their intellectual resources in their efforts to interpret it. Hence it is unwarranted to divide the intelligence of a religious individual into two aspects, as if only one aspect of it were devoted to the search for a knowledge of ultimate reality. The entire intellectual resources of a religious individual are devoted to this search, since the search is, for him, a grave undertaking in which he is constantly aware that it is a fearful thing to do less than he ought in any aspect of his life in relation to the reality supreme in importance above every other reality.

Any belief about such a reality is a concept, and the vehicle of a concept is a symbol, or a set of symbols. A belief that God is the ultimate reality upon which the physical world and human life are ultimately dependent is one sense of the theistic symbol. An individual who believes this is therefore dissatisfied with a metaphysic such as Marcion's, which affirms that there are two ultimate realities, or two Gods, one of which is "subject to error, mistakes, and regrets." Unable to believe that all reality can ultimately be accounted for in terms of one God whose nature is unqualifiedly trustworthy, Marcion proposed the dualistic metaphysic of two gods. But as a Christian, he specifically endeavored to interpret the religious significance of Christ as a revelation of the "good" God. Since the good God revealed by Christ was not, according to Marcion, the Creator of the physical world, the Christian Church was confronted with a metaphysic incompatible with its faith. Hence its opposition to the Gnosticism of Marcion in its unwavering conviction that there is "One God, the Creator."[26]

When religious life achieves the level of spiritual development capable of revering one reality supremely worthy to be trusted, it rejects as incompatible with its faith any philosophy which qualifies the ultimate nature of that reality. It is this spiritual inability of Christian faith to tolerate a philosophy which qualifies the ultimate trustworthiness of Christ which accounts for the sustained efforts within the Christian Church to repudiate the doctrines of Marcion, as well as those of Arius. The motive, for example, of Alexander, Bishop of Alexandria, in repudiating Marcion and Arius was to preserve the ultimate status of the reality in which a Christian trusts as the supremely dependable "Light which lighteth every man that cometh into the world."[27]

The specific faith that Christ is the "Light of lights" makes any subordination of Christ to a more ultimate reality incompatible with the religious belief that the one reality supremely worthy to be trusted is not subordinate in significance to any other reality. Alexander, therefore, rightly opposed the Arian doctrine that Christ is not ultimate, and his opposition to Arius is likewise not merely a philosophical matter. It is essential to Christian faith that Christ is "the Light which lighteth every man that cometh into the world."

As a universally trustworthy authority for life, Christ could not be thought of as subordinate to another authority.

The unique nature of Christian faith is that the reality supremely worthy to be revered for its unqualified trustworthiness is Christ, the Logos, "the Wisdom of God." Thus the point which Alexander made against Arius is essential to the religious significance of Christ for a Christian, since the faith that Christ is the "Light of lights" could not be maintained if the status of Christ was believed to be secondary to a more ultimate reality. This sound point of view which Alexander affirmed was also affirmed by Athanasius in his opposition to the Arians. Stated as a question, it is that "If the Logos (Christ) is mutable, as the Arians consistently maintain, how can He reveal to us the Father, and how can we behold in Him the Father?"

Insofar as Christ is revered as the "Light of lights," the philosophy of Arius is not a defensible foundation for Christian faith. Its indefensibility, however, is not primarily for philosophical reasons, since any point of view may function as a basic premise of a philosophy. It is rather for its incompatibility with the basic premise of religious life that the reality which is alone supremely worthy to be trusted is the ultimate reality. As the supreme authority for Christian life, Christ, the "Light of life," cannot be contingent upon a more ultimate authority. Yet, the Arian point of view is that Christ is not ultimate in authority.

Although one may well acknowledge the soundness of the efforts of Alexander and Athanasius to oppose the view of Arius and the Arians, he must, nevertheless, also be aware that when Arius began his argument with the conviction that there is one God, he distinguished between God and His revelation in Christ. When so stated, the position of Arius is in agreement with the monotheistic position of Alexander and Athanasius, who maintained that "One God is proclaimed in the Holy Scriptures." But believing that Christ is the supreme authority for human life, Athanasius identified Christ with God, and declared that "Christ is God."[28]

Arius, on the other hand, did not identify Christ as "Son of God" with "God the Father," and therefore he maintained the subordinate status of Christ as Son. Yet, for interpreting

Christ as Son, and so as other than God the Father, Arius was condemned by two ecclesiastical assemblies in Egypt, both directed by Alexander, Bishop of Alexandria. Although both Arius and those who opposed him maintained that there is one God, Arius was unable to identify Christ with God after he had interpreted Him as the Son of God. He construed the symbol "the Son of God" to be an acknowledgment that Christ is other than the ultimate Creator, designated by the symbol "God the Father." But since Christ is revered in Christian faith as the "Light of lights," and "Lord of Lords," it was equally inconceivable to Alexander that Christ should be secondary to a more ultimate reality.

Thus affirming the faith in one God, both Alexander and Arius developed philosophies of the nature of God which became incompatible with each other, and which therefore constituted the basis for the long and bitter controversy within the Christian Church. If the faith of Arius had been expressed in the single premise that there is one God, and if the faith of Alexander and Athanasius had remained the single-statement creed that there is "One God," there would have been no Arian controversy in the early Church.

The underlying motive of every Christian who believes that Christ is the "Light which lighteth every man who cometh into the world" is to direct homage to Christ as supremely worthy to be revered as ultimate in significance for human life. This was the motive of Apollinaris of Laodicea who endeavored "to so construct Christology that no shadow of mutability might fall upon Christ."[29] Yet, in his noble effort within the limits of language to make distinctions compatible with Christian faith, Appollinaris maintained that Christ "has two natures," one which is eternal, and one which suffered death. The belief, however, that Christ, "the Light which lighteth every man," should die, is incompatible with the concept of a reality exempt from mutability. Hence, Apollinaris differentiated the mutable historical Jesus from the immutable "Light" or Wisdom of God, and he did so in order to escape the conclusion that God is subject to mutability. Noble as was the motive of Apollinaris, his point of view was, nevertheless, condemned by three councils: two in Rome in A.D. 374 and 376, and one in Constantinople in 381.

The motive underlying the efforts of Apollinaris to preserve Christ from mutability is the very motive underlying the opposition of Alexander and Athanasius to Eusebius. Eusebius, as well as Apollinaris, endeavored to interpret the nature of Christ as Son. But since the concept of "son" implies that there is a prior "father," Eusebius interpreted the status of Christ as subordinate to God the Father. The religious significance of the faith of Eusebius, however, was preserved by his conviction that God is the ultimate reality revealed in Christ. And yet, when the status of Christ as the supreme authority for human life is interpreted in terms of the symbol "son," the connotation "coming after a father in temporal order" was introduced into Eusebius' Christology. Eusebius, therefore, was anathematized on the grounds of introducing the conventional connotation of son into the symbol "son" when referring to Christ. Under the influence of Alexander and Athanasius, a decree was therefore directed against the view of Eusebius. It declared that "the holy and apostolic church anathematizes those who say that there was (a time) when he (Christ) was not."[30] The religious motive for this repudiation of Eusebius is that when Christ is interpreted as the Son he is also interpreted as coming from the Father, and so as "the Son of God is mutable or changeable,"

When men argue a philosophy from a conventional symbol, their philosophy is an expansion of the conventional sense of the symbol. It is this tragic confusion of the conventional connotation of symbols with the aspirations of religious life which accounts for controversies among men of religious faith. There are, however, no grounds for controversy between one religious faith and another insofar as the underlying motive of religious faith is to direct homage to the reality most worthy to be revered. But controversy is inevitable when men forget the motive of religious life, and become preoccupied with the symbol which they use for articulating their faith. It is apparent time and time again in the history of Christian doctrine that controversies arose when individuals gave more attention to symbols than to the reality they sought to interpret by means of symbols.

Peculiar to the Christian faith is the unique significance of Christ. A preoccupation, therefore, with the nature of

Christ is not a secondary matter in a formulation of Christian doctrine. Since, however, Christian faith had its origin in a monotheistic tradition in which the symbol "God" refers to the ultimate reality, the introduction of a second term "Christ" into the vocabulary of religious life gave rise to a problem: How can there be one reality supremely worthy to be worshiped when it is referred to both as God and also as Christ?—especially when Christ is thought of as an historical person, who was born, and who was crucified.

Acknowledging this, a council in Alexandria in A.D. 362 authorized the term "hypostasis" as orthodox terminology for designating an individual nature, or person. Believing that there is more than one individual reality of supreme importance for a Christian, the Council approved as permissible the reference to one god as "three hypostases", "provided these be conceived not as different in nature nor as separate natures."[31]

Since "hypostasis" is defined as "nature," its connotation is thus the same as "ousia." The council at Alexandria thereby recognized the identity of the senses of two words, both of which were occasions for controversy, and accordingly decreed that Christ and God are to be thought of as having the same nature. This identification of the nature of two realities which are nevertheless distinguished as Father and Son is known as the "homoousian" doctrine.

Since the Arians stressed the aspect of the sonship of Christ, they could not also believe that son and father are the same. Their inability to regard a son and a father as the same in nature (*ousia*) led them to maintain the "homoiousian" doctrine, according to which, Christ, as worthy of man's homage, is similar to God who is supremely worthy of man's worship. This point of view implied in the Arian position was most explicitly stated by Euzoius of Antioch (A.D. 361) in the formula: "In all things the Son is unlike the Father."

Yet, when this emphasis is made of the disparity of Christ and God, a Christian is confronted with a problem of what constitutes the fundamental difference between his faith and Hebraic faith, since both believe that there is one God. When Christ is interpreted as "Son of God," a distinction is therefore made between the significance of Christ and God, and Ursacius and Valens endeavored to express this difference in the Third Council of Sirmium by affirming "there is no doubt that the Father is greater."

This Council's endorsement of the Arian view as orthodox was an explicit abrogation of the Nicene Creed as the doctrinal basis of Christian faith. Yet the Arian formula was again reaffirmed in the council at Antioch in A.D. 358, and so, as Professor Seeberg points out, "the terms *homoousios* and *homoiousios* as well, appeared to be banished from the world."[32]

But the banishment of a particular vocabulary is not the resolution of problems which arise in the struggle of religious life to clarify its faith, and to state its faith in understandable language. The same problem, therefore, as had given rise to the first formulations of doctrine, persisted within the Church after the councils of Sirmium and Antioch. The triumph of the Arian point of view at these two councils was, so far as language can make clear, the reassertion of a view which was first maintained in the early Church when Christ was referred to as the Son of God.

Tertullian, who died about one hundred and thirty years before the council of Antioch, had consistently maintained that Christ as the Son "proceeded from God." When these terms are construed in their customary sense, this implies that "He had a beginning." Or stated in another form, "There was a time when . . . the Son was not."[33] And Hippolytus, in developing a Christology on the basis of the conventional connotation of "son," agreed with Tertullian in affirming that "The Father begat the Logos."

The struggle to formulate a doctrine capable of articulating religious faith is a struggle not only of the collective body of a church, but also of every religious individual who endeavors as best he can to understand the nature of the reality supremely worthy to be revered. When, therefore, a Christian believes that Christ is the "Light which lighteth every man," he is anxious to devote the resources of his intelligence to understanding this reality of supreme significance for his life, and so in his own individual life he duplicates the struggle of the collective Church.

The struggle of the Christian Church to formulate a creed

is not, therefore, extrinsic to Christian faith. What is extrinsic to Christian faith are some of the symbols proposed for interpreting the nature of God and the nature of Christ. One thing, certainly, which is not essential to Christian faith is the vocabulary inherited by the Church from Greek philosophy. Since no particular vocabulary is essential to the metaphysic of religious life, the history of Christian doctrine is in part a record of what is not essential to religious life. No particular philosophical terms which entered into the creedal formulations of the Christian Church are indispensable to Christian faith. Eunomius, for example, pointed out that "if the Son is the first creature of the Father, then it follows; that he is neither *homoousios* nor *homoiousios*, since the one indicates a beginning and a division of the nature, and the other an identity. (But) even a similarity is, in regard to the nature, impossible between the Begotten and the Unbegotten."[34]

The term "ousia" likewise is not indispensable to Christian faith, and in the councils at Ariminium and Seleucia (A.D. 359) it was specifically repudiated, "on account of its having been used only by the Fathers, but being unknown among the common people, (it) occasions scandal because the Scriptures do not contain it."[35] Yet the term "ousia" performed one of the critical roles in the history of Christian doctrine, since it was regarded as Sabellian heresy to speak of one *hypostasis* (person) instead of one *ousia* (essence).

The fact that a symbol which is heretical one day may be creedal orthodoxy the next is not an essential feature of religious life. It is rather a characteristic trait of the history of religiously significant symbolism. It would, therefore, not be unjust to point out that some of the controversy over doctrinal formulae was more of an intellectual struggle with symbols than it was a spiritual struggle. And so Theodoret's comment that Eunomius "presented theology as technology" applies to more theologians than just to Eunomius.[36]

Basilides, for example, even denied the religious significance of Jesus by maintaining that it was not he who was crucified, but rather Simon. In so doing, however, he removed from Christian faith the premise which constitutes its unique conviction that God was revealed in a special way in the historical life of Jesus. Praxeas, on the other hand, was determined that the unique significance of Jesus must be maintained at all costs, and he went so far as to argue that God the Father was crucified in the person of Jesus.[37] Noëtus of Smyrna likewise was determined to defend at all costs the belief that historical events in the life of Jesus were not incompatible with His worship as first in the order of religious significance. Arguing that Jesus is God, he concluded that God Himself was born at the birth of Jesus. But in order to maintain this identification of the historical Jesus with the eternal God, he introduced a purely semantic device in proposing that "when the Father had not yet been born, he was rightly called the Father; but when it had pleased him to submit to birth, having been born, he became the Son." In his attempt to defend the religious significance of the historical events in the life of Jesus, Noëtus did not hesitate to attribute mutability to God. In accommodation to his initial identification of events in the life of Jesus with events in the nature of God, he maintained that "the Father also called himself to life again." Thus in attempting to defend the religious significance of the life of Jesus, Noëtus repudiated the very foundation of Christian faith itself, that there is an ultimate reality which is not subject to the mutability either of human life or of the physical world. Noëtus of Smyrna thereby serves as an example of the price which a dialectician will sometimes pay for a verbal solution to a spiritual perplexity.

It would, for example, be difficult to conceive of a more cynical solution to a spiritual perplexity than the Monarchian doctrine that it is only a verbal distinction to speak of the eternal God as "Father" and the historical Jesus as "Son." Yet this was affirmed in declaring that "He who is called Father and Son is one and the same . . . called by name Father and Son according to the figure of the times."[38] When one is aware of this type of solution to a doctrinal problem, he sees that a modern tendency to classify all spiritual perplexities as merely a matter of terminology, and so merely a matter of an arbitrary naming operation, is not so modern as it is often thought to be.

Cynicism toward the struggle of spiritual life to understand the nature of a reality supremely worthy to be worshiped is not, however, a feature of any one historical era. It is an aspect of a type of life which is unable to comprehend the profundity of some of the problems with which religious life struggles in its attempt to interpret the nature of a reality esteemed as first in the order of worthiness to be worshiped, because first in the order of existence.

Some of the problems which arose in the history of Christian doctrine may without injustice be traced to a verbal origin. Dionysius of Alexandria, for example, believed that he successfully resolved the Christian's perplexity about the worthiness of Christ to be worshiped as the ultimate Light of Life by his formula that "We expand the Monity undivided into the Trinity, and again combine the Trinity undiminished into the Monity."[39] Dionysius' intended transition from a reality which is one to a reality which is other than one is, however, only a passage from one word to another word in which the customary senses of the words are ignored.

The verbal character of the formula which Alexander of Alexandria devised in his polemic against Arius is no less obvious. He asserted that "The Son exists unbegottenly in God, always begotten, unbegottenly begotten."[40] Just how far one can go in such a use of language without forfeiting intellectual integrity is certainly a point which may well be debated. But it is perfectly clear that a manipulation of words in total disregard for their ordinary senses contributes in no way to the intellectual clarification of a spiritually significant problem.

One may well wonder how an individual without intellectual scruples in his methods for resolving a spiritual problem can even be aware of the spiritual character of a problem. The formula, for example, "he who is by nature God is *homoousios* (of the same nature) to him who is by nature God"[41] is purely verbal, although its verbal character may be partially concealed by the Greek term. When this term is removed, the formula is obviously the repetitious statement, "he who is by nature God is by nature God," and as tautological, this statement affirms nothing. It is simply an assertion about the consistency with which terms are used. Referring to no reality external to verbal usage, the statement, therefore, has no religious significance, even though the word "God" may be included in the terminology.

When individuals are overcome by intellectual fatigue in clarifying their spiritual perplexities, they often find an easy way to resolve their problems by a purely verbal solution. One of the most commonly used of such solutions is the paradox, an example of which was proposed by John of Damascus when he maintained that there is "one deity . . . united without mixture and continuously separated." What is especially disappointing about this formula is not its total disregard for any customary sense of conventional terms, but the fact that it "marks the close of the (doctrinal) controversy in the East."[48] It is almost heartbreaking that this purely verbal solution should culminate six hundred years of doctrinal controversy in the Christian Church.

If one were to say no more than this, he might well be suspected of a cynical attitude toward the efforts of the Christian Church to articulate in an intellectually acceptable manner the basic convictions of its faith. In order, therefore, to escape such a cynical estimate, one must first distinguish between the spiritual struggle of human life to understand the nature of the ultimate reality it endeavors to worship and its intellectual struggle to select symbols appropriate for expressing the faith which motivates the struggle.

When one distinguishes between a spiritual struggle to know an ultimate reality and the intellectual effort to articulate interpretations of it, he becomes aware that this twofold aspect of religious life is not unique to the Christian Church. It is rather a feature of all religious life which endeavors to articulate its faith by means of symbols. The selection of symbols for expressing religious faith is an intellectual responsibility with which religious individuals are confronted when they endeavor to interpret the reality they revere as supremely worthy of their worship. This intellectual responsibility consequently is an aspect of every religious life which endeavors to express its faith in some intelligible form.

The ancient Babylonians, for example, believed that there is one ultimate creator of the world, whom they called Merodach. They also believed that there are other realities which are likewise religiously significant, and of which men must take account. The realities other than the creator which were believed to be of religious significance are "the illuminator of night," "the god of righteous things," "the god of lordship and domination." Each of these realities was accordingly given a name. "The illuminator of night" was called "Sin"; "the god of righteous things" was called "Samas"; "the god of lordship and domination" was called "Bel." Thus the religious Babylonian was confronted with the problem of the relationship of Sin, Samas, Bel, and Merodach. Convinced that there is one ultimate reality, referred to as Merodach, he concluded that Sin, Samas, and Bel are modes of Merodach.[43]

Another example of such theological modalism may be found in the ancient Hittite religion, which affirmed the belief that although there is one supreme god, called the "Weather God," there are, nevertheless, other realities of utmost significance in man's life. Such realities are "The God of the Thunder," "of the Lightning," "of the Clouds," "of the Rain," "of the Meadows," "of the Palaces," "of the Army," and "of Peace." Believing that there is one supreme reality, called the Weather God, and also believing that there are many realities of religious significance in man's life, the ancient Hittite proposed the modalistic concept as a means for reconciling his religious faith in one supreme reality with his acknowledgment that there are many realities upon which he is also dependent. This modalistic concept for the Hittite is that "there are many special forms of the Weather God." These are the "Weather God of the Thunder," the "Weather God of the Lightning," the "Weather God of the Clouds," etc.[44]

Basic, therefore, to the concept of a Triune God interpreted as "three persons in one Godhead" is a philosophical premise which differs in no essential respect from the premise basic to Babylonian and Hittite theologies. "The three one in divinity, and the one three in individualities"[45] is thus a concept which is not unique to any one religion or any one theology. What is peculiar to a particular theology is the symbolic means for expressing the interpretations of the ultimate reality and its multiple manifestations.

According to Hittite theology, there are not only "different

Weather Gods," but there are also "different Sun-Gods," and these "special Sun-Gods," Professor Güterbock says, are "to be considered as distinct divine personalities." When, however, he maintains that they are "distinct divine personalities rather than mere aspects of one and the same God"[46] it may well be that he superimposes upon Hittite religion a non-modalistic theology.

The writers of the ancient Vedas, no less than the Babylonians and the Hittites, were faced with this same problem of the relation of one ultimate reality to other realities of religious significance. Agni, for example, was esteemed as the god of fire, and the manifestations of his nature were acknowledged in the altar-fires and in hearth fires. One of the Vedic hymns affirms that Agni is "of like appearance in many places," and another declares that "there is only one Agni though many times kindled."[47] The Zoroastrian believes both that Ahura Mazda is the "supreme god," "the Lord, the All-knowing One," "the creator and sustainer of the world of good," and also that there are "other divine beings" interpreted as "sons and daughters of Mazda," which as Professor Finegan says, are sometimes "spoken of as created by him" and at other times "treated as personified qualities of his nature."[48]

Interpreters of religion are faced with the problem whether a particular religious faith affirms that there is one ultimate reality which is manifested in multiple modes, or whether there is one ultimate reality which created subordinate realities. In interpreting the Hittite religion, for example, Professor Güterbock acknowledges this problem by saying, "The question arises whether these are individual deities or only different manifestations of one and the same god."[49]

The people of prehistoric Crete "worshiped a Goddess known by the name of Eileithyia," esteemed as the "patron of the Nether Regions, of fertility, and of the domestic cult." She was also worshiped under the forms of "the Goddess of Healing, the Goddess of War, and the Goddess of the Seas." The relationship between Eileithyia, therefore, and the many other goddesses of significance in the religious life of the Minoan-Mycenaean people constitutes a problem for an interpreter of the religion of this ancient culture. "Whether all these Goddesses should be considered as one Great Goddess with different functions or a number of independent and separate divinities each characterized by a particular function remains," as Professor Mylonas acknowledges, "still to be determined."[50]

This alternative with which an interpreter of religions is faced is also an alternative with which religious faith itself is faced when it endeavors to interpret the relation of religiously significant realities to one ultimate reality. The existence of an ultimate reality is not problematic for religious faith, since religious faith is the conviction that there is an ultimate reality which is supremely worthy of man's trust. But an interpretation of the relation of this one ultimate reality to other religiously significant realities is a problem for a reflective religious life.

When this relation is interpreted by a Christian Monarchian, for example, it is maintained that "Father and Son is one and the same . . . called by the name Father and Son according to the figure of the times."[51] This Monarchian monotheistic faith is likewise basic to Sabellian and Arian theologies which affirm that "We know only one God, Unbegotten," who "alone is unoriginated . . . without beginning."[52] Hence the unwillingness to compromise a monotheistic faith in order to account for the religious significance of the historical Jesus gave rise to the Sabellian point of view that "Father, Son, and Spirit are only different designations of the same person, corresponding to the degree and form of his revelation."[53] According to Sabellius, there is one ultimate reality, but several symbols for designating it. Yet, in the use of the several symbols, it is acknowledged that one reality is manifested in several forms designated by the symbols "Father," "Son," and "Spirit."

It was not only the Monarchians, the Sabellians, and the Arians who were unwilling to compromise their religious faith in one ultimate God. Marcellus and Athanasius were also unwilling to do so. Marcellus, Bishop of Ancyra, "one of the most zealous of the Nicene party," maintained that we are "not to divide the divine Being."[54] Athanasius likewise affirmed that "One God is proclaimed in the Holy Scriptures," and argued that "we are not to think of 'three hypostases separated from one another' (since this) would lead to Polytheism."[55] Thus in his determined effort to avoid any doctrinal expression compatible with polytheism, he defended the theological premise that there is "one divine nature," whether it be referred to by the philosophical term "ousia" or "hypostasis."

When, however, one ultimate reality is affirmed as the basic premise of Christian faith, a Christian is confronted with the problem of differentiating his faith from the faith of the Old Testament prophets, who also were uncompromising in their monotheism. It is this problem which motivated the Cappadocians to affirm that there are three divine *hypostases* but one divine *ousia*.[56]

Thus the pendulum of intellectual effort in formulating theological doctrine swings within the scope of this fundamental problem of how one ultimate reality retains its unity, or identity, when it is revealed, or expressed. So long as there is a mind capable of formulating an interpretation of the ultimate reality, just so long will there be an effort comparable to the doctrinal traditions of the Christian Church, of the Babylonians, the Hittites, the Hindus, the Minoan-Mycenaean peoples, the Zoroastrians—to enumerate only those already mentioned. All of these doctrinal traditions testify to a spiritual struggle to express a faith that there is one ultimate reality, supremely worthy of man's worship, and yet there are also other realities of religious significance for human life.

While acknowledging the utmost significance of Christ as the "Light which lighteth every man that cometh into the world," St. Augustine never compromised his faith that there is "one God, and one God in the same sense as one Creator." Yet, in order to avoid the abstract unity of one god, which would be incompatible with the faith that He who is the Creator is also the "Light which lighteth every man," St. Augustine refers to God as the Trinity. But profoundly aware that every symbol for interpreting the nature of God is man's creation, St. Augustine acknowledged the insufficiency of human symbolism for articulating the mystery of the ultimate

One. "When it is asked," says St. Augustine, "What are the three? human speech at once toils with great insufficiency. Yet we say three persons, not in order to express it, but in order not to be silent."[59]

Chapter Five

THE RELIGIOUS INTERPRETATION OF SYMBOLS

1. *A religious interpretation of symbols rests upon a metaphysic*

A symbol is any man-made device which directs attention to a reality other than itself; and a symbol which directs man's attention to the reality he reveres as the ultimate determiner of his life is religiously significant. The function, therefore, of a religious symbol is its religious meaning; which is its role in directing man's reverent attention to the reality upon which he acknowledges his ultimate dependence. Hence there are no physical criteria for what constitutes a religiously significant symbol. The religious significance of any object is the function it performs in reverently directing an individual's attention to the reality he esteems as ultimate in the order of existence. The ceremonial vessels cast in China during the Shang civilization, for example, performed this function. In no way representing the reality believed to be ultimate in the order of existence, they, nevertheless, were means for directing man's homage to such a reality. "Dedicated to the Great God known in China as the Soil-god,"[1] they thus performed a unique symbolic role. Free from all attempts to represent a deity, they are "aniconic," and insofar as they were the principal symbols of early Chinese religious life, this early period in the history of Chinese religion may be classified as "aniconism."

An awareness of an immediate dependence upon parents is likewise basic to the religious life of the Chinese, and it dominates their life as it does not dominate the life of many other people. Thus the ritual function of early Chinese bronzes is not confined only to acknowledging an ultimate dependence upon the God of the Soil. It extends also to acknowledging a direct dependence upon ancestors. The religious function of altars and altar vessels among the early Chinese is, therefore, to acknowledge dependence upon realities determinative of the source of life and its continued sustenance.

Any reality of utmost significance for life may become religiously significant. Food is one such reality. Parents are another. Life cannot be sustained without food, and without parents, there can be no life. Hence a comparable significance of the fertility of soil and parents underlies the acknowledgment in ancient Chinese religion of man's final dependence upon an ultimate determiner of all life.

A division of Chinese religious rituals into two categories is not, however, fundamentally different from a division of emphasis in any religion where more than one reality is acknowledged to be of outstanding significance. If one remembers the long struggle within the Christian Church to acknowledge the supreme significance of the ultimate Creator and the "Light that lighteth every man," he is able to appreciate the similarity of the problem of religious life wherever it occurs in selecting symbols adequate for expressing man's faith. The problem of creating symbols for acknowledging man's ultimate dependence is a problem with which all reflective life is faced. It is the necessity of acknowledging every reality of utmost significance in life, and yet doing so without compromising the basic conviction that there is one reality upon which every other reality is ultimately dependent.

The Chinese awareness of the difference between a pictorial representation and an ultimate reality goes back to an early origin. One recorded prohibition against the use of images is at least as old as the earliest teachings of Confucius. Although Confucianism "does not properly permit the use of images," in accommodation, nevertheless, to the inability of many people to think of a reality of supreme significance apart from some concrete form, "a change has taken place in the course of time"[2] so that images now appear even in Confucian temples.

The ancient Chinese caution against images expresses a clear awareness of a universal tendency to confine attention to the image, and so lose its significance as a symbol. The preference, therefore, among the early Chinese for aniconic ritual vessels and tablets expresses a profound awareness of the ease with which the human mind slips from the symbolic role of an object to the physical features of the object itself. It is this same sound understanding of the ease with which a mind loses the symbolic function of an object that accounts for Empedocles' repudiation of the pictorial images in early Greek religions. He declares: "It is not possible to draw near (to God) even with the eyes, or to take hold of him with our hands . . . for he has no human head fitted to a body, . . . but he is sacred and ineffable."[3] Xenophanes likewise criticized the crude anthropomorphism in Homer and Hesiod, declaring that "God is one . . . not like mortals in body or in mind." This same awareness of the limitations of all pictorial imagery for representing the ultimate reality continues throughout the history of Greek philosophy, and continues into the history of the Christian Church, accounting for many of the problems with which the Church Fathers wrestled.

An awareness of the inadequacy of every symbolic device for representing the nature of the ultimate reality underlies the *Summa Theologica*. St. Thomas declares that "'no created form can be the likeness representing the essence of God to the seer,"[4] and so to presume "to know God by any created likeness is not to know the essence of God."[5] Since God is transcendent of human life and the physical world, there is no object within human life and the physical world which can adequately represent His nature. Hence, according to St. Thomas, no object can represent God "even generically."[6] Human life and the physical world are creations of God, and as such, they perform the role of signs in religious life, referring to their Creator. But their reference is aniconic: they do not represent His complete nature, but refer to only one aspect of His creativity.

One may acknowledge the inadequacy of all objects for representing the nature of God, without, however, also maintaining that there are no objects suitable for referring to the ultimate reality. According to the Psalmist, the Heavens do not represent the full nature of God, but they are signs of His glory in the cosmic role of Creator.

When Aristotle spoke of the "inspired utterance" of the Ancients, he had in mind this same distinction between a sign for designating God and the reality of God, as first in the order of cosmic importance. But, as Aristotle points out, when the belief about "the divine (which) encloses the whole of nature" was handed down "in mythical form,"[7] it became identified with the image embodying the belief; and in the identification of this profound belief with a pictorial image, the belief itself became adjusted to the limited capacities of individuals for comprehending the spiritual significance of the ultimate reality.

The belief that there is an ultimate reality, transcendent of human life and the physical world, is the "inspired utterance" whose religious significance cannot be reduced to the symbolic vehicle of any representative image. Whatever device man uses for directing his worship to this ultimate reality performs a symbolic role without, however, presuming to represent the ultimate reality. A distinction, therefore, must always be made between a device intended to direct man's worship to the ultimate reality, and a symbol presumed to portray the ultimate reality.

A caution in the use of symbols in religious life is not, however, a repudiation of the use of symbols in religious life. Even an acknowledgment that there is an ultimate reality is a distinction between the physical world and a reality transcendent of it, and such a distinction constitutes a basic part of the sense of all religious symbols. Hence it is of no service to religious life to repudiate symbols, since without some symbols there can be no religious interpretation either of human life or of the physical world.[8]

Caution must be exercised not only in selecting symbols for performing a religious role. It must also be exercised in a philosophy of symbolism. It is easy to go to extremes, and when some individuals realize that the ultimate reality cannot be represented in any concrete form, they conclude that all symbols are antithetical to religious life. This conclusion, therefore, reveals a fundamental misunderstanding of the nature of symbolism, and yet, such a mistake is commonly made when people disparage every symbol for interpreting the nature of God.[9] It must always be remembered that symbols may be used for interpreting the nature of God without being used to represent His nature.

2. *A religious interpretation presupposes some sort of dualistic distinction*

There would be no motive for man to turn beyond his resources to another reality if every requirement of his life were fulfilled within his own resources. There would likewise be no ground for orienting his life to a reality other than the physical world if the physical world included everything he required for the fulfillment of all his needs. The religious Apache, for example, acknowledges his dependence upon the "Child of the Water" which he reveres as the ultimate source of all the goods he cherishes. Although his symbol for designating this ultimate reality reveals a primitive tendency to think in terms of a pictograph, the religious sense of his symbol is not peculiar to primitive life. It is a feature characteristic of all religious life. This characteristic of all religious life is the faith that there is a reality apart from the physical world and human life which is the ultimate source of all goods worthy to be cherished in human life.

Just as there is no religious life without a reference beyond the resources of human life and the physical world, so there is no religious life without some distinction between the significance of the physical world and a reality transcendent of it. This distinction between the physical order in which man lives and a source of good which is other than the physical world is essential to religious life. What is not always clear to religious life is an interpretation of the nature of the ultimate source of good. But what is clear to religious life is that the physical order in which man lives does not include every good worthy to be desired, and its acknowledged insufficiency motivates a religious individual to turn beyond the physical order and the resources of his life. Yet such an orientation of life would never be sustained unless an individual were convinced that there is a reality other than the physical world to which he may turn for a help he cannot secure in the physical world. Some distinction between the physical world and a reality other than it is clear to religious life, although what is not equally clear to religious life, primitive or civilized, is the specific relation between the insufficiency of the physical world and an ultimate reality believed to be its final determiner.

A basic conviction of religious life is that there is an ultimate reality upon which the physical world depends, and yet, this very conviction confronts religious life with a perplexing problem of reconciling the faith that the world which depends for its nature upon the ultimate reality is itself inadequate for the fulfillment of man's needs. The Apache, for example, believes that the "Child of the Water" created man and the physical world, and yet, he also acknowledges that men suffer. His faith that there is an ultimate reality worthy to be worshiped for its goodness is not, therefore, discredited by his acknowledgment of the multiple evils with which he is beset in the world, since the fact of evil in the physical world does not constitute the religious motive for believing there is a reality other than the physical world. Man turns beyond the physical world because he believes there is a reality transcendent of it which can contribute to his life what the physical world cannot. A failure, however, to conceive of a *completely* trustworthy reality transcendent of human life and the physical world is not primarily a religious failure. It is an intellectual failure. It is an inability to dissociate one reality from another. Millions of the people in India, for example, trust in goddesses believed to be benevolent and protective. And yet, these goddesses are also feared because they are believed when offended to be capable of causing the very diseases from which men turn to them for help. Mariamma is such a goddess, trusted in the villages of the Tamil country for protecting men against smallpox, and yet also feared as the source of this disease. Thus due to an intellectual failure to abstract the nature of a deity from realities in the physical world, these people are unable to conceive of a reality unqualifiedly trustworthy, even though transcendent of the physical world.

It cannot be denied that a radical dualistic metaphysic confronts religious faith with a perplexing problem. But it likewise cannot be denied that it also preserves religious faith from a weakening which is inevitable when a supremely trustworthy reality is not distinguished from every other reality whose worthiness to be trusted is only partial. A factor responsible for weakening religious faith is any qualification in the trustworthiness of the reality to which religious life turns for a dependable help. The Egyptians, for example, struggled with the desert which made inroads upon their fertile fields. Hence the contest between the desert and the cultivated fields conditioned their interpretation of the symbols of religious significance. The fertility of the soil was believed to be dependent upon the benevolent nature of Osiris, whereas the blighting effects of the desert were believed to be results of the evil Seth. This particular distinction made by the Egyptians was thus accomplished by means of a dualistic metaphysic, which has not been maintained with consistency throughout the religious life of India. Contrasts within the physical order in which the Egyptians lived contributed no small amount to the clarification of their dualistic metaphysic, and so to the radically different senses of two of their religiously significant symbols. That there is some correlation between the physical context in which men live and the nature of their concepts is a sound premise, although how extensive this correlation may be is problematic. But it is significant that the Zoroastrian metaphysic is a dualism no less clearly defined than the Egyptian. The radical contrast between Ahura Mazda, the source of good, and Angra Mainyu, the source of evil, may thus in part be accounted for by the geographical parallel of Iran and Egypt. But whatever the explanation may be, a Zoroastrian preserved his faith in the goodness of Ahura Mazda by differentiating the ultimate source of good from any deficiency whatsoever. In identifying evil with one source, symbolized by Angra Mainyu, the Zoroastrian sustained his religious faith in the unqualified trustworthiness of Ahura Mazda.

The radical distinctions between Osiris and Seth, as well as between Ahura Mazda and Angra Mainyu are instances of symbolic means for preserving metaphysical distinctions in some way essential to religious life. But it is not essential to religious life that the source of evil should be pictorially interpreted in a personified form. Evils may be acknowledged as a fact in human life even when they are not interpreted in terms of a dramatic imagery. "In Hittite texts," for example, "evil is never imagined in the form of evil demons."[10] Hittite symbolism in this regard differs from Babylonian symbolism, but integral to the metaphysic of Hittite religion, just as to Babylonian religion, is a clear awareness that there is an essential difference between what is unqualifiedly worthy of trust, and what is not.

Religious life is a turning from the physical and human contexts in which man lives because they are insufficient for the fulfillment of all of his requirements. Their inadequacy to fulfill his requirements does not, however, account for his conviction that there is a reality transcendent of them. His conviction that there is such a reality is the unique contribution of his religious faith to his life.

It is not only contrasting events in the physical world which constitute a basis for dualistic distinctions in religious symbolism. Contrasting features in human life are also occasions for a dualistic interpretation, and so for dualistic distinctions in religious symbolism. Among dualistic sets of Chinese symbols are the terms *Yang* and *Ying*, *shen* and *kwei*, *huen* and *poh*. Although the senses of these terms differ, they nevertheless fulfill comparable symbolic functions. *Yang* and *Ying* designate opposite cosmic forces. *Shen* and *kwei* designate personified cosmic powers. *Huen* and *poh* designate qualitatively different substances, one superior, and the other inferior.[11] But common to these sets of terms are opposite senses. And it is the opposite senses of these terms which make them suitable as symbolic devices for expressing an interpretation of radically unlike types of human behavior. Although referring to a person by a single name is an acknowledgment that he is one reality, an individual at times questions the warrant for assuming that there is one person throughout radically differing behaviors. Thus in interpreting human nature, one is faced with a problem comparable to the problem faced in interpreting the physical world. A sea which at one time destroys a village with violence may at another time be as placid as an inland water. The sun which gently warms the earth one season burns it to a desert the next. The very difference between thirst and relief from thirst, or the difference between hunger and relief from hunger, are contrasts with which everyone is early acquainted in his life. And throughout his life he is constantly confronted with comparable contrasts, often of great violence. Violent contrasts both in physical nature and in human nature therefore constitute a perplexing problem for reflection. But one thing is clear: a minimum condition for thinking about such radically contrasting phenomena is a symbolism consisting of at least two opposite senses.

One formulates a philosophy in order to clarify a problem, and yet, a philosophy itself may become a problem. A Zoroastrian, for example, who believes that the ultimate source of the physical world and of human life is "the Lord, the All-knowing One," is, nevertheless, faced with many features of the physical world and human life which challenge his belief. It is for this reason that he distinguishes so clearly between Ahura Mazda, "the Lord, the All-knowing One," and the many subordinate beings, the *asura-ahura*. Hence a Zoroastrian who affirms a monotheistic belief also thinks in some form of dualism, although it may not be "fully elucidated" into a doctrine of Angra Mainyu as "the spirit of evil."[12]

One of the spiritual struggles of life is to dissociate the nature of good from the nature of all that stands in contrast to it; and without this distinction, there is neither a serious moral life nor a serious religious life. Such a serious moral and religious life is thus repudiated by a philosophical premise that "good and bad are one."[13] A struggle to acknowledge fundamental differences with which man is confronted in his life, and also to believe that there is an ultimate source of all realities is clearly manifested even within the history of Hindu religion. The most ancient of Hindu faiths is that Varuna is the Supreme Creator, and as such, is other than the physical world. But in the course of time, Hindu sects minimized the radical distinction between the physical world and a reality other than it, which is free from evil, as the physical world is not.

Although Hinduism has traditionally been classified as a pantheism, there have, nevertheless, been tendencies away from pantheism, among which are the efforts of Sankara in the eight century A.D. Another Hindu religious philosopher of the early twelfth century A.D. was Ramanuja, who also specifically affirms that "We know from Scripture that there is a Supreme Person whose nature is absolute . . . goodness; who is fundamentally antagonistic to all evil . . . who differs in nature from all other beings . . . who is immeasurably raised above all possibility of anyone being equal or superior to him; whose name is the highest Brahman."[14]

An ability clearly to distinguish one reality from other realities is an intellectual capacity to think of one reality as essentially different from other realities, and this intellectual capacity is an essential condition for the particular religious faith that there is one reality radically unlike every other reality. Religious faith, however, as a universal expression of human life is not confined to this clear dualistic distinction. If one were, therefore, to maintain that a clearly defined dualism is essential to religious life, he would make religion contingent upon a particular type of metaphysic. And the argument throughout this essay is that this procedure is indefensible. The history of Hinduism includes thousands of years between the early Aryan concept of the one supreme Varuna, or Brahman, and the reaffirmation by Sankara and Ramanuja that Brahman is "absolute goodness," supreme above every other reality, and so of a nature unlike every other reality.

It would be indefensible to press into one metaphysical category the entire history of Hinduism, which extends from the dawn of civilization to the present. And it would be no less indefensible to press into one metaphysical category the interpretations of the ultimate reality basic to all the religions of mankind. This becomes clear if one is to classify Zen Buddhism as a religion. According to it, "Zen is the ocean, Zen is the air, Zen is the mountain, Zen is thunder, and lightning, the spring flower, summer heat, and winter snow."[15] The very interpretation of so many distinguishable realities in the physical world in terms of Zen makes one aware, however, that Zen is not the same as the physical world. The predication of Zen to the ocean, the air, the mountain, the thunder, the lightning, as well as to man himself, makes it clear that Zen is something other than each of these distinguishable realities, although their religious significance for a Zen Buddhist cannot be understood except in terms of Zen.

When one first reads the assertion that "Zen is the ocean, Zen is the air" etc., his immediate response is to deny the religious significance of Zen. But when he becomes aware that each distinguishable aspect of the physical world, as well as of human life, is included in Zen, he sees that Zen may be an ultimate reality which is of unique religious significance for a mystical type of life. One must always remember that language is an instrument for the clarification of man's interpretations of the nature of life and the context in which he lives. To permit language, therefore, to constitute a hindrance to the enlightened understanding of another person's point of view would be a grave misuse of language. One would do well always to remember, as Aristotle has reminded us, that "articulate speech is a luxury," whose purpose is to serve "its possessor's well-being."[16]

Just as the peculiarities of language must not be allowed to handicap an intelligent understanding of the religious faith of people whose culture is other than one's own, so the peculiarities of human mentality must not be permitted to obstruct an understanding of what is essentially religious in the life of peoples of vastly differing intelligence. Primitive men, for example, do not clearly distinguish between animate and inanimate realities; between sense experiences and dreams; between body and soul. Since mental images are often as vivid in dreaming experiences as they are in sensory perceptions, a primitive person makes no clear distinction between these two aspects of his life. Mirages and hallucinations which occur during the hours he is awake are thus not classified in a category distinct from his dreams. Since in his dreams he has a clear image of a deceased member of the family, he does not distinguish between the dead and the living as does a civilized person. When it is realized, therefore, that some of the distinctions which are basic to a civilized mentality are not equally basic to a primitive mentality, it must likewise be realized that some features of civilized religious life should not be expected to be found among all primitive religious life.

An ability to distinguish between waking and dreaming experiences, for example, is taken for granted among civilized people. It is not taken for granted among primitive people. The distinction between the animate and the inanimate is a primary differentiation for civilized men. It is not for primitive men. Hence the distinction between a reality which a primitive religious individual trusts and the realities he does not trust is likewise not so clear as are the distinctions made by civilized religious individuals, whose mental capacities do not remain so undeveloped as do those of primitive people.

Primitive people do not make distinctions between human life and animal life as civilized people do. The Bataks of Sumatra, for example, believe they descended from animals, and after death will again return into animal form. The Apaches believe that the Coyote was once able to speak as human beings. Since for many people there is no clear distinction between men and animals, it would be a mistake to stipulate a particular type of dualistic philosophy as essential to religious life. It would be a mistake, for example, to define religion as a belief in a personal survival after death, or in a personal immortality. This belief presupposes a dualistic distinction between life and afterlife, as well as between body and soul. But there are many people who do not think in terms of such a dualism. It would, therefore, be indefensible to stipulate a mental achievement as essential to religious life when it is peculiar only to a particular level of intellectual development.

A failure to distinguish body and soul, human life and animal life, is not, however, peculiar to primitive life. Some of the most literate of men maintain essentially the same belief as do primitive men. An ancient belief in the transmigration of life from one form to another, for example, presupposes no radical distinction between human life and animal life. And some of the most learned and sensitive of men have believed in transmigration. One need mention only Pythagoras, and Socrates, possibly Plato, and for certain Plutarch.

Whether a failure to make a distinction between animal life and human life accounts for the belief in a passage from animals into men, and from men into animals, or whether the observed similarity of men and animals in so many aspects of life accounts for a belief in transmigration, is a problem which obviously cannot be resolved apart from sheer dogmatism. In the tradition of Hindu mysticism, for instance, the human self is never regarded as a distinct identity. Hence a traditional Hindu distinction between man and the physical world is in no way comparable to a traditional Christian dualistic metaphysic of the self and the physical world. Insofar, therefore, as a particular type of dualistic distinction is insisted upon as essential to religious life, the number of people regarded as religious would be far less than is customarily assumed. Although there is certainly a basis for classifying the thought of Gautama as religious, the basis for doing so is obviously not his concept of the self as an identity persisting into another life. And insofar as some form of transmigration is implied in his concept of *karma,* there likewise is no clear distinction between human life and animal life. Thus if original Buddhism is to be included in the category of religion, it cannot be on the basis of any dualistic distinction between animal life and human life, any more than it can be on the basis of a metaphysic of a personal immortality, as is common in Western philosophy.

If the distinction between human life and animal life is to be maintained as essential to a religious interpretation of the nature of man, Egyptian belief must likewise be rejected from the category of religion, since major deities in Egyptian culture are represented as half animal and half human. Anubis, a deity of the Underworld, for example, is represented with the head of a jackal. Thoth, a supranatural being who conducts the dead to the Underworld, is represented with the head of an ibis. One may go on and on enumerating the peculiarities of the religiously significant symbols of the Egyptians. But the purpose would be only to make clear that a dualistic distinction between human life and animal life is not basic to Egyptian religion. This specific dualistic distinction, therefore, may not be stipulated as essential to religion, although it is a feature of some religions.

Religious faith is not a philosophy of the nature of human life, or the human soul, or even of the destiny of human life. It is an affirmation about the existence of a reality which is supremely worthy of man's trust, both in this life, and in another—whatever such a life may be. What makes the faith of Socrates, for example, specifically religious is not his particular philosophy of the self. It is his conviction that whether man lives beyond this present life or not, there is an eternal God, a knowledge and reverence of Whom constitutes the supreme good in this life, and also the supremely worthy preparation for any status of one's nature after this life.

3. *Religious symbolism reflects what man regards as most significant in life*

The religious significance of a symbol is the meaning which man associates with it. Every religious symbol, consequently, reveals in some way man's scale of values, since what he most values supplies the sense for the symbols in his religious life. Any symbol has religious significance for an individual when it designates a reality he believes is transcendent of human life and the physical world, provided he esteems the reality for its pre-eminent importance in his life. But the specific sense which a symbol has for an individual is limited to his capacities for comprehending what is spiritually significant. When, for example, fertility of the soil, of cattle, and of human life is a dominant concern, the imagery in which a people interprets the nature and the role of a supranatural reality is in images associated with the various aspects of birth and growth. When the scope of human life enlarges to include interests which are not confined to birth and sheer survival, associations with religious signs also enlarge to include realities which are not confined to the animal basis of life. Only after the horizons of human life extend beyond the restricted range of instinctive interests do the heavenly bodies, for example, become signs of supreme significance in religious life. The concept of "Lord of Heaven" as a reality of pre-eminent importance in life could not emerge as a spiritual achievement when man's interests are confined to purely animal problems. The symbols of Varuna for the Hindus, Zeus for the Greeks, Jupiter for the Romans, are records, therefore, of spiritual achievements in expanding the scope of human life beyond the range of animal preoccupations.

The concept of a supreme god of the sky is a spiritual achievement, however, which is not peculiar only to civilized people, since it is not specifically a function of culture, but rather of the scope of an individual's interests. When an individual's interests are not confined to the most elementary of concerns, the range of his attention is likewise not restricted to the most rudimentary problems of animal life. Even the Bantus, who are primitive by every standard of cultural achievement, conceive of a god of the sky. There is, therefore, no fundamental reason why the Bantus' concept of a god of the sky should not be as spiritually significant as the ancient Sumerians' god of the sky, Anu; or the ancient Egyptians' goddess of the sky, Nut; or the ancient Chinese deity of the heavens, Shang-ti.

The reality of supreme religious significance is not just any object of pre-eminent importance for an individual. It is only a reality believed to be other than man's life and his resources, as well as other than the physical world. Because it is regarded as ultimately determinative of his life, of his resources, and of the physical world, it is revered as pre-eminent in cosmic significance. One would not, therefore, include a "deification of the sun"[17] as a religious act. He would also not speak, as Socrates does, of the "gods in whom many foreigners believe—sun, moon, earth, stars, and sky."[18]

The physical sun may well be a sign for a deity, as it is for the Egyptian Amon-Ra, but the physical sun is not the ultimate reality for the worshipers of Amon-Ra. When men regard the physical sun, or the physical moon, as of pre-eminent spiritual significance, their reverence should be classified as an instance of naturism. When one distinguishes naturism from religion, he thereby distinguishes religious reverence from a non-religious reverence. When the intended referent of utmost reverence is an object within the physical world, reverence is not religious.[19] The intended referent of religious life is a reality other than the physical world.

Since the only objects which man can use as signs are within reach of his vision and his touch, it is understandable why signs which refer beyond the physical world must, nevertheless, be themselves objects in the physical world. Chuang Tzu, the Taoist philosopher of the fourth century B.C., made a clear distinction between physical nature and the Tao when he declared that "a contemplation of the silent vastness of nature is of extreme importance" "on the road toward union with Tao." Nature thus performs a unique religious function for the Taoist sage, who "sitting by the sun and the moon, and holding the universe in his arm," contemplates the Tao, which is other than the physical universe. But this contemplative use of Nature should not be spoken of as a worship of Nature. It is a reverence for a reality other than Nature, as it is manifested in Nature. Thus Nature for a contemplative Taoist, who lives "in the depths of the country,"[20] is a sign of a reality other than itself.

If every reverent attention directed to an object in the physical world were to be classified as "religious," religion would include many forms of superstition. To prevent this indiscriminate classification, the essential features of religious faith must be kept in mind. When religious life includes all that men do to revere a reality believed to be ultimate, and other than the physical world, the category of religion performs a distinct function in interpreting human life. When, however, every act of respectful attention is classified as religious, it is impossible to understand the unique nature of religion.

If a difference is to be made between superstitious practices and religious practices, a distinction must, therefore, be made between the superstitious significance of realities in the physical world and their religious significance. Mountains have always been impressive to men, and for this reason have been regarded with awe. It is, consequently, understandable why mountains often are classified as objects of worship. Mountains have had a special significance, for example, in the history of China, and so have played "an important part in the religious life of the Chinese."[21] According to an ancient tradition, for example, the mother of Confucius prayed to a mountain, and as a consequence, Confucius was born.[22] While there is no justification for doubting the genuineness of the reverence of the mother of Confucius for a mountain, there is, however, real justification for raising a question of the religious character of such reverence. If reverence itself constitutes the criterion of religious life, religion becomes a function of a type of feeling or attitude. But the criterion of religious significance is in part also metaphysical. The metaphysic of religious faith is the conviction that a reality other than the physical world is alone supremely worthy of trust, and so of reverence. When this specific metaphysic is basic to reverence, reverence is religious. It is religious, therefore, not on the grounds of man's attitude and feeling alone, but also on the grounds of his deliberate adjustment to a reality esteemed for its unique status in existence.

The reverent attitude of the mother of Confucius as recorded in tradition must, consequently, be classified in some category other than religion. One need not doubt that the birth of a son may well have been the most important event in her life, and one likewise need not doubt that she directed as genuine a reverence to the mountain as has ever been directed to a deity. But if the term "religion" is to be used for identifying a unique type of human life, its sense must also be unique, and its unique sense is preserved only when the reality to which reverent attention is directed is regarded as supremely trustworthy, such as objects in the physical world are not.

One must bear in mind two distinguishable types of interpretation in any classification of religious behavior. One is the interpretation by a person who classifies a behavior as "religious." The other is the interpretation by a person who is classified as "religious"; and the difference between these interpretations may account for some of the misunderstandings about religious life. Dr. Ackerman, for example, points out that "In Mongolia today supernatural powers are addressed by heaping up conical mounds of stones." According to this interpretation, mounds of stone are not worshiped. They are regarded rather as symbolic of supranatural powers which are worshiped. Thus two entirely different points of view are possible for an interpreter of Mongolian practices.

Whether or not a classification of behavior is sound depends upon the accuracy with which an individual understands the point of view of a person whose behavior he presumes to classify. A competent study of religions presupposes, therefore, an ability to understand motivation. Religious motivation is an endeavor to do all that one reverently can do to acknowledge his dependence upon a reality he esteems as pre-eminently dependable, because ultimate in the hierarchy of existence. A religious individual may employ any type of device in acknowledging his dependence upon such a reality. But the function of such a device must always be symbolic. It must refer to the reality believed to be ultimate in the order of reality.

Mountains, and especially mountain peaks, have had a special significance for human beings throughout human history. A "cult of the mountain peaks," for example, flourished among pre-historic Greeks; and even in later Greek history, mountain peaks were represented in art forms as realities of utmost importance. When a mountain was interpreted as a sign of the "Goddess of the Mountains," the mountain performed a unique role in religious life. Hence when a mound of stones referred to a mountain, it also performed a religious role by virtue of the transfer of the religious significance of a mountain to the symbol for the mountain.

The symbolic form for representing a sacred mountain was artistically refined in the course of cultural development. Instead of crude mounds of stones, temples were built with columns cut from stone. A symbol of the earliest of Greek sanctuaries, for example, was "a great stone portal," and "the place of the column could sometimes be taken by a mound," or by a conical heap of stones. Such "sacred columns" served a twofold function. One was "as the material home for the spiritual being." The other was "the aniconic representation of a divinity."[24] In either case, the temple was interpreted by religious people as a symbol referring beyond itself. The early Greek temple, therefore, was religiously significant, not by virtue of its architecture, but by virtue of its symbolic function.

The difference between a mound of stone, a column, and a temple is artistic. It is not necessarily religious. Artifacts are man's creations, but the reality to which man directs his worship is not his creation. Insofar as artifacts differ in their effectiveness in performing this symbolic role, they differ also in their religious significance. But the religious significance of any artifact is never its artistic merit. It is rather its symbolic capacity for directing worship to the ultimate reality, whose unique status is its pre-eminent worthiness to be worshiped.

Professor Güterbock points out that "Mountain cults have been known in Anatolia through the ages," and he interprets Hittite texts to refer to mountains "either as independent gods or satellites of the Weather God."[25] The significance of mountains for the Hittites, according to this interpreter, is thus twofold. One is religious, and the other is not. Reverence for a mountain as such is not religious, although it may well be as earnest as any religious reverence is. The Hittites' reverence for mountains as "satellites of the Weather God" may justifiably be classified as religious, not, however, by virtue of their earnestness, but by virtue of the metaphysic which underlies it. A mountain as a physical object is not pre-eminently worthy to be worshiped. There may be any number of factors accounting for the awe with which men revere it, but awe and reverence as such are not criteria of religious experience. Professor Otto and those who follow him maintain they are. But the point of view maintained in this essay is an uncompromising criticism of their position.

The awe and reverence which men have for mountains may well be classified as religious experiences when men esteem mountains as signs of a reality whose majesty they only suggest. The Scriptural account of Moses in "the wilderness of Sinai," going "up unto God" in the mountain is an account of such a religious experience. The Scriptural statement that "the Lord called unto him out of the mountain" can in no way, therefore, be confused with a worship of a mountain. The religious significance of Mount Sinai in Old Testament history is clearly its sign-function.

When rivers are regarded as signs for a supernatural reality, they acquire religious significance comparable to mountains. But the religious significance of a river, like the religious significance of a mountain, depends upon its role as a sign. This sign-function of a river is made clear in the Chinese term for floods, *chu lung*, which means "to send forth the dragon."[26] This distinction between a river and a reality other than a river, believed to be responsible for the flooding of a river, is a sign-distinction. It is a distinction between a physical river and a reality believed to be ultimately in control of a river. The dragon-symbol has additional religious significance, since the dragon for the Chinese has from the most remote of ages been a symbol of cosmic power.

A comparable religious significance is associated with the Brahmaputra. As the son of Brahma, this great Indian river is looked upon as a sign of reality other than the river itself, and other than the physical order of reality. The Egyptians associated a comparable significance with the Nile. Insofar as their dependence upon the Nile was a reminder to them of their total dependence upon the ultimate creator of the Nile, the Nile performed for them the role of a religious sign, and it was construed as such a sign when they interpreted it as the creation of Amon-Ra. The Nile itself may well have been an object of reverence, homage, and sacrifice. But in so far as it was, such reverence, homage, and sacrifice were not religious, notwithstanding their earnestness.

A common mistake in a study of religion may be traced to the influence of those who identify the sense of mystery and awe with the essence of religious experience. The religious significance of the Nile was not an expression of the Egyptians' awe and reverence, but of their clear understanding of their ultimate dependence upon the reality upon which the Nile itself depends for its existence and for its ordered cycle. The religious significance of the Nile in the history of the Egyptians is, therefore, not primarily its mystery, due to man's failure to understand its origin, and its periodic recession. It is rather its role as a sign for directing man's reverence to the ultimate reality upon which he acknowledges his own final dependence for all that sustains his life.

Mountains and rivers may well perform the role of signs in religious life, directing men to a reality other than the physical world. But mountains and rivers have grave limitations as symbols of religious significance. Although capable of directing reverence to a reality transcendent of the physical world, the specific significance of such a reality is always conditioned in part by the senses of the symbols which refer to it. The majesty of a mountain, for example, may be a concrete means for designating a reality whose majesty exceeds in every respect the physical mountain. But when majesty is the primary connotation of a mountain as a religiously significant sign, it is also a primary feature associated with the nature of the ultimate reality. When, however, a religious individual thinks of the ultimate reality not only in terms of majesty, but also as the authority for human life, the feature of majesty is not religiously sufficient. A belief, for example, basic to the Old Testament is that the ultimate reality is not only the Creator of the world, but is also "the God of Israel," "the Lord which calls thee by thy name."[27] A symbol for deity derived from a physical mountain is, therefore, not adequate for expressing a religious faith of this type, since there is no feature of a mountain, notwithstanding its majesty, which can suggest the role of an ultimate authority for man's life. Man may be awed by an ultimate reality to which the majesty of a mountain refers, but majesty is not the primary element in a final moral authority.

When man reveres the ultimate reality as his Creator and Sustainer, as well as the final authority for his life, he is, therefore, faced with a problem of selecting symbols adequate for acknowledging such significance for his life. Since such significance cannot be acknowledged in symbols whose sense is simply majesty and power, the symbol of a mountain, notwithstanding its majesty, and the symbol of a river, notwithstanding its power, are not adequate for fulfilling this symbolic function required by religious life. A mountain or a river is not an adequate symbolic vehicle for a faith in "the Lord (which) called thee in righteousness"; which will "keep thee, and give thee for a convenant of the people, for a light"; "to open the blind eyes, to bring forth the prisoners from the prison, and them that sit in darkness out of the prison house." Notwithstanding the majesty which a physical mountain may contribute to the sense of a symbol referring to the ultimate Creator, it cannot connote the authority of such a Creator for man's life. "He that created the heavens, and stretched them out, he that spread forth the earth" may well be designated by a sign such as the majesty of mountains. But when this same Creator is also revered as the ultimate authority by which all men ought to live, the role of His significance in human life cannot even be remotely suggested by the feature of majesty. It is this role of God, however, which Isaiah acknowledges in declaring that He who created the heavens and the earth is also "He that giveth breath unto the people upon it, and spirit to them that walk therein."

Development in the spiritual refinement of human life makes some symbols inadequate for the religious role of referring to the ultimate reality. When, therefore, a religious individual is faced with the problem of selecting a symbol adequate for interpreting the nature of an ultimate reality, he is faced with a spiritual problem, and a problem in symbolism. An individual who believes that the ultimate reality is also the ultimate authority for life does not acquire his religious faith from symbols. But desirous of clarifying his faith, he wrestles with the problem of finding suitable symbols. It is at this point in the spiritual history of religious life that men become aware of the religious inadequacy of purely natural signs, and of symbols whose sense is derived from purely natural objects. It is, therefore, at this point that natural signs for a supranatural reality are supplemented by signs which connote life, even when they are not displaced by them. It is at this point, consequently, that zoomorphic and anthropomorphic signs emerge into religious life to fulfill a function which aniconic signs cannot fulfill.

A symbol, such as a swastika, which is not a representation of anything, does not, therefore, function in the same way as does an image of an ideal person. Although "the swastika is frequently seen upon the breast (of Buddha)" as "the ancient symbol of cosmic unity, inner peace, and holiness,"[28] it does not of itself bring about an awareness in a worshiper's life of such religiously significant achievements. It is only when the swastika is given the sense of "inner peace" that such peace is connoted by it. But "the half-closed eyes" of a figure of Buddha reflect, without additional commentary, "a wonderfully deep inner peace and harmony." Hence, as Dr. Reichelt points out, "seeing these figures tells better than many words what there really is in the Buddhist dogma of Nirvana, and in the concept of 'Buddha.'" Any meaning whatsoever may be read into a sign, but when an arbitrary association is made between a sign and its sense, the sign does not itself connote the sense. The sense must first be read into the sign. The partially-opened eyes of a figure of Buddha, on the other hand, immediately connote the ideal of Buddhist faith, and constitute a concrete reassurance to a devout Buddhist that spiritual aspiration can be rewarded by spiritual achievement.

The limitations of aniconic signs, or objects which do not represent, was early acknowledged in the history of religious symbolism. It is this acknowledgment of the inadequacy of non-representative objects which accounts for man's early efforts "in transforming the earlier aniconic beliefs into anthropomorphic conceptions,"[29] or even into zoomorphic representations. But the transition from non-representing devices to those which presume to represent features of deity is certainly not without profound problems. No object which man makes can more than indicate what religious life acknowledges of the "glory (due) unto the Lord." Hence man must always be cautious of the role his creations assume in his religious life, lest his reverence be misdirected to an adoration of "graven images."[36] The gravity of this problem becomes clear when one becomes aware that every sign and every symbol with which man refers to the ultimate reality has a sense which is given it by man himself. Hence the role of sign or symbol in religious life is conditioned by the spiritual development of religious life.

Although capable of thinking of a reality other than the

physical world, the Apache is so limited in his symbolic equipment for interpreting the significance of this reality that he thinks of it in terms of a coyote, and puts statements into the mouth of a coyote which other religious people attribute to the ultimate Creator. The coyote, according to the Apache, performs the same role, for example, which God performs according to the writer of *Genesis*. It is Coyote who "looked about everywhere," and "whatever he thought of became so." When Coyote thought that green hills should appear, they "extended upward everywhere": "Beautiful hills with all sorts of green plants growing on them came into existence."[31] The religious faith recorded in the first chapter of *Genesis* is that "God said, 'Let the earth bring forth grass, the herb yielding seed, and the fruit tree yielding fruit after his kind. . . . And the earth brought forth grass and herb yielding seed after his kind."

It would be a mistake to ignore the difference in the actual zoomorphic symbol of the primitive Apache and the anthropomorphic symbol of the writer of *Genesis*, but it would be equally a mistake to ignore the basic concept which underlies these two accounts of creation. The reality ultimately responsible for creating the earth is, according to both, other than the earth, and the supranatural character of this reality is suggested by means of the symbolic pictograph of creating by mere word. This creation by fiat is in part the sense of the symbol "God" for the writer of *Genesis*, and it is also in part the religious sense of the symbol "Coyote" for the Apache.

The writer of *Genesis* did not put the creative fiat into the mouth of an animal since the significance of an animal for him is not the significance of an animal for the Apache. The symbolic function of the coyote for the Apache, however, is the same function which is performed by the symbol "God" for the writer of *Genesis*. If, therefore, the actual symbols which men use are to constitute criteria for classifying religious faith, the category of religion will be inclusive only of the cultures whose symbols coincide with the symbols an individual himself prefers. But when the intended function of a symbol is taken into account, the actual symbol is not of primary religious significance. What is of primary religious significance are the senses of symbols, and the senses of religiously significant symbols are interpretations of an ultimate reality and of man's final dependence upon it.

Some inhabitants of India today do not hesitate to represent Siva by the sign of a pig; Indra by the sign of a bull; the sun-god Surya by the sign of a horse or a goat. Within the restricted limits of their spiritual development it is common for many to think of Hanuman, the monkey-god, as having ultimate significance for their life. Inconceivable as this association of an animal with an ultimately significant reality may be, the association, nevertheless, is made by millions of people. If their restricted spiritual development, therefore, were to disqualify them from the classification of "religious," one would have to alter his concept of religion to make it fundamentally a function of culture. But when people who revere deities represented by animals do all they conceive as worthy for acknowledging their dependence upon a reality ultimately determinative of their life, they are religious by virtue of their faith, and not by virtue of the peculiarities of their symbols.

When one recalls the early history of Hinduism, and remembers the exalted sense of the concept of Varuna, as God of the Heavens; or remembers the ancient sense of the symbol Brahman, as the ultimate source of the physical world and human life, he cannot help being bewildered by the latitude within which spiritual sensitivities develop, and also with the latitude within which they deteriorate. Whatever the explanation may be for this deterioration in the role of religiously significant symbols, it is a fact that such specific deterioration has occurred in some sects of Hinduism. It may well be that the "luxuriance of animal life in India from pre-Aryan times" accounts for "the many forms of the cult of animals"; or it may be that "the enervating influence of the climate with its moist heat, especially in the Ganges basin,"[32] accounts for this phenomenon. But whatever the explanation, the significant fact for a philosophy of religion and a philosophy of symbolism is that any object may be selected as the sign or symbolic vehicle for conveying a meaning. The meaning of a sign or a symbol for an individual is thus the "mental content" which is associated with it, and this content reveals the level of man's spiritual sensitivity and his intellectual development. An individual who is insensitive enough to select a pig or a monkey as a sign, or even a representation of deity, may be religious insofar as he acknowledges his dependence upon a reality he reveres as an ultimate determiner of all he cherishes in life. That some people are able to comprehend the role of such an ultimately significant reality within the confines of a symbol of a pig or a monkey does not repudiate the fact of their religious acknowledgment. It merely indicates what a spiritually undeveloped life regards as compatible with a religious acknowledgment of dependence upon an ultimate reality. A primitive Andaman Islander, for example, finds nothing inappropriate in interpreting the moon as coming to the earth in the form of a pig. His concept indicates not only his total ignorance of the nature of the moon, but also something of his general insensitivity. Only the most insensitive of human life could associate a pig with the same heavenly body which has inspired men throughout the ages with the loftiest of sentiments. Thus the Andaman Islanders' indentification of an embodiment of the moon with a pig indicates how some concepts, and so some symbols, reveal the spiritual level of human life.

If, however, religion did not comprehend every form of human culture, it would not be a universal human phenomenon. The inclusion of every type of culture within the category of religious life may constitute a problem. But the definition of religion in a way which delimits it to particular types of culture constitutes another problem which is even more disturbing in its implications.

When man articulates an interpretation of conditions essential for his life, it is understandable that a reality with which he is most familiar should be selected as the symbolic vehicle of his interpretation. The ancient Canaanites acknowledged their ultimate dependence upon Baal as the reality upon which "the earth relied for its fertility,"[33] and so they designated the fertility-significance of Baal by the symbol of a bull. The Hittites likewise regarded the bull as a sacred animal because they believed it was cherished by the Weather God, whom they revered as the ultimate determiner of the growth of crops, and so the reality upon which human life ultimately depends. The Hittites also believed the stag was an embodiment of the fertility of the fields, and for them it was a symbol of the ultimate determiner of fertility. The Hittites did not, however, acknowledge their ultimate dependence upon a particular stag roaming wild in the fields. As Professor Güterbock points out, "the animal never stands for the god himself."[34] No religious sign ever does.

Any so-called worship of an animal cannot, therefore, be included within the category of religion, even in its most rudimentary form. When, however, the "God of the Fields" is revered as the reality upon which men are ultimately dependent for the fertility of their fields and cattle, then the sign-function of an animal is compatible with a religious interpretation. Any object may perform a sign-function or a symbolic-role in religious life when men are clear about a distinction between the reality upon which they acknowledge their ultimate dependence and the signs or symbols by which they refer to such a reality.

"The Weather God in the form of a bull" is not an identification of the Weather God with a bull. It is a distinction between two realities. One is a reality upon which man acknowledges his ultimate dependence, and the other is a means for designating this reality. Thus it is one thing to speak of "the Weather God in the form of a bull," and another thing to speak of "bull worship." The distinction between these two statements is, however, often disregarded, and in consequence, every conceivable superstitious rite is identified with religion. In consequence of this identification of superstition with religion, religion itself is often regarded as one instance of superstition. The distinction, therefore, between a sign and a reality it designates is basic to any distinction between religion and superstition. There is no religion without a distinction between a reality transcendent of the physical world which is worshiped, and the means by which it is worshiped. A most important distinction between symbol and symbolized reality is, consequently, glossed over insofar as reverence for the bull is regarded as "bull worship." That the bull may well have been treated with utmost regard by agricultural peoples, out of whose culture the ancient civilization of the Near East arose, cannot be denied. It is denied not only in order to be consistent with the definition of religion in this study as all that man does to acknowledge his dependence upon a reality transcendent of the physical world. It is denied also on the basis of a principle of symbolism essential to religious reverence, in distinction to other types of reverence. If a reverence for an animal is classified as worship, then a fundamental distinction must in turn be made between a worship which is religious and a worship which is not religious.

The Algonquins refer to the Supreme Being as "The Great Hare." The Hopi refer to it as the "Plumed Serpent." A choice of such symbols for designating the reality which is revered for its ultimate significance may well be an occasion for spiritual distress. But such distress is partially quieted when one remembers the fundamental principle of all religious symbolism: The reality with which man is most impressed in his life becomes for him the symbol by means of which he interprets the reality he reveres for its ultimate significance. If, therefore, the Algonquin's and the Hopi's reverence is to be construed as a worship of a rabbit and a serpent, it must be classified in some category other than religion. One such category may be zoolatry, as a particular type of idolatry. But just as idolatry should not be included in a history of religion, so neither should zoolatry be included in a history of religious symbolism. A worship of an animal, as if it were the reality of ultimate significance, just as a worship of an image, as if it were the reality of ultimate significance, is not religious, no matter how earnest man's reverence for either may be. The referent of religious worship is a reality esteemed for its ultimate significance, because other than the physical world, and other than any object within the physical world.

Chapter Six

DEPENDENCE ON THE SYMBOL

1. *Religiously significant signs and symbols reflect man's scale of values*

Signs and symbols have religious significance by virtue of their reference to the reality upon which individuals acknowledge their final dependence, and the clarity with which individuals are aware of their final dependence upon an ultimate reality is one measure of the genuineness of their religious faith. Although an awareness of dependence is a mark of the genuineness of religious faith, it, nevertheless, presents a perplexing problem in reflecting upon the worthiness of some signs and symbols for assuming religious significance. Almost every object of which people of the dynamistic or animistic level of religious development are aware is thought of as an embodiment of power. It is this type of mentality, therefore, which accounts for the tendency among millions of people living in India today to treat almost every object in their lives as influenced by a deity, or dependent upon a deity. Every product of the farm, for example, is thought of in terms of such a reality. Buttermilk is an occasion for acknowledging dependence upon Challalamma, the goddess believed to preside over it. A cart is an occasion for acknowledging dependence upon Balamma, goddess of the cart. Thus a complete catalogue of the gods and goddesses among the primitive villagers of modern India would constitute an inventory of every object of significance in their lives. Since these many gods and goddesses are assumed to perform specific functions in man's life, they are commonly classified as "functional deities."

One of the functional deities of the ancient Romans, for example, was thought of as having ultimate jurisdiction over thorny plants. Since the Latin term for thorn is *spina*, this Roman deity was called *Spinensis*, and his special role was thought of as assisting the Roman farmer in rooting out vegetation with thorns. So concrete were the expressions of religious interpretation among the agricultural people of ancient Rome that a special deity was even thought of as ultimately determinative of the fertilizing function of a dunghill. This deity was called *Sterculius*, whose name derives from *stercus*, the Latin term for dung. This particular example from Roman life is not mentioned to disparage a religious interpretation. It is mentioned only as an instance of a problem. There is no religious life apart from man's acknowledgment of his final dependence upon an ultimate reality for the goods in life which he cherishes. But when every detail of life becomes an object of religious significance, an individual is faced with the problem of considering the limits which religious life itself ought to impose upon its own value scale.

When, for example, buttermilk, carts, dunghills, are thought of in terms of deities, man tends to think of every object in his life as of equal religious significance. When he is not morally and intellectually developed sufficiently to think in terms of one reality of pre-eminent significance in his life, he is also unable to organize the goods of his life into a hierarchy of values. And conversely, when he is not capable of distinguishing between objects on the basis of their comparative significance, he is also incapable of associating pre-eminent significance with one object in distinction to the lesser significance of all other objects.

Although intellectual deficiencies are inevitably revealed in religious life, they are not necessary features of it. They are features of it only insofar as they condition its development and expression. Man's failure to distinguish between the comparative significance of valued objects is basic to primitive polydaimonism—a type of religious life in which man acknowledges his dependence upon as many realities as there are objects of significance in his life. Since every aspect of his life has some object with which it is especially associated, the number of such significant realities is as large as is the number of particular details in life to which he gives his attention.

Although polydaimonism is not a universal category of religious life, it, nevertheless, expresses a type of mentality with which one is constantly faced in attempting to decide whether or not such concepts as the Indian goddess of the cart, the Lithuanian goddess of the bees, and the Roman god of the dunghill should even be included in the category of historical religion. The answer, of course, is that they must be included by virtue of the role they perform in the lives of these people. But just as the scale of values peculiar to the Indian villager, the Lithuanian peasant, and the Roman farmer is not the scale of values of every person, so every person's religious life is not on the same level as these people who are bound so closely to the concrete details involved in their struggle for sustenance.

2. *What man values is reflected in his religious ritual*

The motivation of religious life is acknowledging dependence upon a reality believed to be ultimately determinative of the goods in life which an individual cherishes, and whatever he does to acknowledge his dependence is, when organized into a pattern, a religious ritual. Thus a religious ritual may be defined as a pattern of acting which an individual believes is a worthy means for acknowledging his dependence upon the reality he reveres as pre-eminent in the order of reality. Religious ritual, consequently, includes every conceivable form of behavior in human history which men have considered worthy for acknowledging their dependence upon the reality they regard as pre-eminent in the order of importance for their life, because unique in the order of existence. Religious motivation is, therefore, always commensurate with intellectual and moral development, since what an individual regards as worthy of doing in relation to the reality he reveres for its pre-eminent importance is his worship, and rituals are among the vehicles of his worship.

"The ever-arduous task of keeping fed" accounts for the motivation in primitive societies to do all that is believed to be appropriate for securing food. A restriction of religious motivation to seeking food is not, however, a universal feature of religious life. It is a predominant feature of religious life, and so of religious ritual, only when men are faced with the almost total uncertainty of their food supply, and this extreme uncertainty of the availability of food for some people accounts for their preoccupation with ritualistic attempts to control the factors in the physical context connected in one way or another with their food. But all men who are clearly aware that they cannot completely control the availability of their food by means of their own resources are aware of their dependent nature, and what they do to acknowledge their dependent status in relation to a reality they trust for its dependability is their specifically religious ritual.

The extreme helplessness of some people in controlling even the most rudimentary requirements for their sheer survival, such as food, is acknowledged in all that they do to relate themselves to a reality they believe can supplement their resources. Hence "The Power must be forever sought"[1] which is believed to be the ultimate determiner of food. This motivation underlies the ancient cave-paintings in which animals were graphically portrayed on the assumption that they could be controlled by means of pictorial representations. The presumption that a representation is actually effective in a real hunt is, of course, a manifestation of ignorance. But particular instances of ignorance are not essential to human life, and for this reason do not occur throughout human history. They are characteristic of certain cultures, although they are not confined to the most primitive of them. Even the civilized Egyptian, for example, profusely painted the walls of his temples and tombs with ritualistically significant objects, just as primitive men painted the walls of caverns and caves with ritualistically significant objects.

The religious significance of ritual is its intended role. Assumed to be effective for relating man to a reality upon which he is ultimately dependent, it is consequently not treated as arbitrary, but as an indispensable means essential to his life. Having such importance, it is, therefore, understandable that rituals once developed are preserved by every means at man's disposal. One means for their preservation is the cultus. The derivation of this term from the Latin term *cultus,* meaning "care," helps one to understand not only the function of a cultus, but also its origin. Derived in turn from *colere,* which means "to cultivate," the term furnishes a further clue for understanding the role of a cultus in religion. Its specifically religious role is its effectiveness for cultivating man's relation to the reality upon which he is aware of his final dependence.

The formation of a cultus is inevitable when the most important aspect of religious life is taking special account of realities upon which man is dependent for his life. It is thus inevitable as an expression of the seriousness with which man acknowledges his confrontation by a reality revered as the ultimate determiner of all that he cherishes. When a reality has this pre-eminent significance, it is consequently revered as other realities are not. This differentiation, therefore, between realities of differing significance is basic to religious rites, and so is basic also to the earnest endeavor of religious life to preserve them for their utmost significance.

A record of all that men have believed is effective for preserving what they consider to be of utmost help in acknowledging their final dependence upon an ultimate reality would be a history of the religious cults of human life. The cult of Soma, for example, became exceedingly complicated because so many details were believed to be of significance for acknowledging dependence upon the determiner of the properties of the soma plant. According to Professor Farquhar, "the historical taproot of the Rigveda" may be traced to the many hymns included in this ancient cult.[2]

Rituals which have developed in the history of mankind reflect peculiarities of geographical and cultural contexts. What is unique to particular totem rituals, for example, is peculiar to certain localities. When, therefore, one understands how geographical factors have entered into the cults of primitive life, he sees how arbitrary some of the Freudian interpretations of totemism are. There is no one universal motive underlying totemism as cults. There are various motives, one of which is food. The Kangaroo Men of Australia, for example, depend upon the kangaroo for their survival.

Hence for them, the kangaroo is a reality of utmost importance, and its totem is a symbolic acknowledgment of its utmost importance.[3]

Some communities are dependent upon particular types of plants and animals for their sustenance, and whatever people in these communities do to assure their availability becomes a standardized pattern of ritual. A ritual becomes standardized, however, only when the pattern of ceremonial behavior is preserved. Standardizing and preserving a ritual is, therefore, an ancient social responsibility, and the specific social means by which this has been done is the cultus.

The assumed indispensability of a ritual for the well-being of a community cannot be thought of apart from penalties imposed for its disregard. Thus any stipulation of the limits within which men must respect a totem plant, or a totem animal, is the basis for taboos. The term "taboo," or "tabu," is a Polynesian word for designating any object of special significance, either because of its assumed danger to human life, or because of its presumed benefit for human life.[4] The specific role of taboo in primitive life is intended to protect men against the consequences of disrespecting a reality believed to be of utmost significance for their lives. Thus taboos are associated with all religious rites. The restraints of taboos are associated with religious ritual, not because religious rituals are feared, but because their significance is respected. Respect for a ritual as a means by which man enters into a unique relation with a reality of pre-eminent importance involves also a fear of consequences believed to be entailed should he fail to treat the ritual with a respect it is due by virtue of its unique function. The more clearly man is aware of his ultimate dependence upon a reality to which he is related through a ritual, the more is he also aware that the ritual is not merely an optional adjunct to an arbitrary ceremony.

A ritual is religiously significant when it performs the unique role of relating individuals to the reality upon which they acknowledge their ultimate dependence. It is, consequently, essential in a religious life when it is believed to be indispensable for relating an individual to the reality upon which he acknowledges his final dependence. It would, however, be a mistake to maintain that any specific ritual is essential to religious life. The final test of the religious significance of a ritual is the role it performs in religious life. This criterion is not a feature of the physical ritual: It is what the ritual does in relating a religious individual to the reality upon which he acknowledges his ultimate dependence.

A mere acknowledgment of an ultimate reality, however, is not a religious experience. Hence the function of a religious ritual is not the same as the designative function of a language symbol. Its role is not optional, as is the case in the use of language symbols. It is essential insofar as it is instrumental in relating an individual to the reality upon which he acknowledges his ultimate dependence. Thus it is essential by virtue of the function it performs. The criterion, therefore, of the religious significance of a ritual is specifically religious: It is what it does in religious life which cannot be equally done by any other means.

A ritual is always specific because its role is to secure a specific help. One of the most elementary of all human concerns is that there may be food sufficient for one's family; for himself; and for the community. This, for example, is the predominant concern of the Pueblo Indians. Hence "their ceremonials are primarily for bringing rain and fertility." Believed to be indispensable in relating them to the reality ultimately determinative of rain, and so of the fertility of the soil, their ritual has for them the significance of food itself. This transition from man's dependence upon food to his dependence upon a ritual believed to be indispensable in relating him to the reality ultimately determinative of its availability accounts for the utmost significance of the rain ritual in the religious life of the Pueblo Indians.

A person is religious by virtue of what he does in acknowledging his dependence upon a reality he esteems as more worthy of his trust than either the physical world or the resources of human life. Thus a primary concern of a religious individual is with the means by which he relates himself to the reality he supremely trusts. The Eskimo, just as the Pueblo Indian, is preoccupied with the uncertainty of his food supply. A predominant part of his religious life, consequently, is with the means by which he relates himself to the reality he trusts for its supreme dependability. Hence the scrupulous care with which he performs his ritual. A scrupulous concern with ritual, however, is an aspect not only of primitive religion. It is an aspect of every religion in which man is clearly aware that it is a matter of grave significance what he does in relation to the reality upon which he is totally dependent.

Every good in man's life which makes him aware of his final dependence may become religiously significant. The early Romans' awareness of the significance of a family, for example, accounts for their ritual of pouring a libation to the "Genius of the Paterfamilias."[5] The ancient Canaanites likewise believed that their well-being was correlated with the welfare of the community. Hence for them, religion was "a public institution," and what was of fundamental concern in the performance of their religious ritual was "not the family but the household, not the population, but the city."[6] Since corporate welfare was believed to be at stake in the performance of their religious ritual, they did not regard themselves as responsible citizens unless they respectfully did their part in the ritual "directed towards the periodic revitalization of this (corporate) entity." Since a Canaanite was concerned with more than his own well-being, his participation in the collective ritual was not only a moral responsibility. It was also an ethical responsibility, because he was concerned with the welfare of the community. But the significance of ritual for him was not alone ethical, since he believed the welfare of the community was dependent upon a reality more ultimate than the corporate group. It was thus specifically religious insofar as he acknowledged that corporate welfare is ultimately dependent upon a reality transcendent of human life, human possessions, and the physical world.

Every detail in a ritual easily acquires the significance of the ritual itself. It is for this reason that what appears to an outsider to be arbitrary in a ritual has a very different significance for the individual in whose life the ritual performs a role of utmost importance. Ancestral figures among the Chinese, for example, had a ritual significance in the family cult which cannot be appreciated until one understands the significance of ancestors in the pattern of Chinese family life. An ancestral figure has specific religious significance insofar as it is an element in the cultus of family reverence for ancestral spirits, which are believed to be ultimately determinative of the well-being of a family. The indissoluble dependence of individual well-being upon the welfare of a community is expressed in one way or another throughout the world. The Orphics, for example, performed rites "on behalf of departed relatives." The primitive people of Australia developed a "form of totemism which is fundamentally an heroic cult" for acknowledging the influence of ancestors over one's life, and is "found with some variations over most" of the island continent.[7]

Every aspect of human life which is recognized to be of utmost importance may become significant in religious ritual. All human life is faced with an ever imminent injury, and with an unavoidable suffering from disease. Hence men in every stage of human culture have done what they believe is helpful for reducing such hazards with which life is almost constantly confronted. The ancient Sumerians, for example, recited "multitudes of incantations" for the purpose of controlling "the cause of disease." Burning figures of wax or wood believed to represent "the cause of disease" was also a part of their ritual. The Azande of Africa consult a special oracle on the occasion of "the sickness of any member of the family," and their specific means for doing this is by placing branches of different trees in a termite mound. The prognosis of the disease is then believed to be determinable by interpreting the manner in which the termites eat the branches.[8] The Apaches scrupulously respect a multitude of herbs, rocks, and minerals they regard as "medicines which are holy." This same concern with the restoration of health underlies the Navahos' "use of ritual to cure the individual." One of their rituals is the "unraveling ceremony" which consists of a set number of "unravelers" who unwind a string that has been wound around bundles of herbs. This unraveling rite is applied to the afflicted part of the patient's body, symbolizing "release from harm, 'untying' and dissipation of evil."[9]

The helplessness of human life accounts for the earnestness with which religious rites have been performed, although men's ignorance accounts for some of the forms of these rites.

Men are religious when they acknowledge their dependence upon a reality they trust as they do not trust their own possessions, or any object in the physical world; and every device which they use in acknowledging their dependence is religiously significant. Hence ritual in one form or another is world-wide, and so integral is it to religious life that religion is not infrequently identified with it. From the fact, for example, that Confucius "was always wont to set up sacrificial vessels in his childish play," it has commonly been inferred that he "manifested special religious interest."[10] The warrant for this inference may well be questioned, since a ritual is specifically religious only when it is a means for relating an individual to a reality upon which he acknowledges his final dependence. Any performance may become standardized into a ritual, but unless the ritual is a means respected for its unique role in relating man to the reality upon which he acknowledges his final dependence, it is not religiously significant. One may not, therefore, presume to infer the motive underlying a ritual from the performance of a ritual, and he may likewise not presume to infer from an individual's participation in a ritual the individual's attitude toward it. A ritual may be an aspect of religious life; and it may also not be. Religious life is possible without ritual, since man may acknowledge his dependence by means other than ritual. A "contrite heart" is one such way. Thus it would be indefensible to define religion in terms of ritual, but it would be equally indefensible to look upon ritual as unessential to religion. Whether it is essential or not depends upon the role it performs.

A ritual is religiously significant only as symbolic, referring to a reality other than itself. Thus any aspect of human life may be associated with a religiously significant ritual; but when it is, the role of ritual is the same. It is to relate man to the reality he reveres as pre-eminent in importance. The transition from youth to adulthood, for example, is one such event in human life which is not only socially significant, but also religiously significant. A person by virtue of his maturity enters into a new set of responsibilities, and a ritualistic acknowledgment of this transition from youth to adulthood is one way of taking into account responsibilities with which he is confronted as a member of a community. But the specifically religious significance of a ritual associated with puberty is an acknowledgment that an individual in this difficult capacity is faced with obligations for the fulfillment of which his abilities are insufficient. Hence a ritual performs a religious role when it relates him to the reality he trusts for its ultimate dependability in supplementing his own abilities. Thus it is not the ritual which makes an individual's acting specifically religious. It is rather the motivation of a religious individual to do what he can by means of a ritual in relating himself to an ultimately dependable reality upon which he acknowledges his final dependence.

The particular aspect of life which becomes an occasion for a religious acknowledgment of dependence and trust determines the form of a ritual. Thus a ritual associated with the passage from childhood to adulthood is patterned after actual birth. Passing into a new role is consequently thought of in terms of being born into a new life, which is thought of in terms of a new person, and "in some cases the dramatic representation of it is made to resemble in various details the actual birth from the mother."[11]

The specific religious significance of a ritual for an individual is determined by the function it performs in relating him to the reality he reveres for its pre-eminent importance in his life. The religious significance of baptism, according to St. Paul, is, for example, the birth of man into a new order of living: "like as Christ was raised from the dead by the glory of the Father, so we also should walk in newness of life."[12] But if the achievement of so important an end in life were believed to be dependent entirely upon ritual, ritual would be a form of magic, and not of religion. The new life, according to St. Paul, is made possible "by the glory of the Father." The difference, therefore, between a religious ritual and a magical rite is a difference in the reality believed to be effective for enabling man to achieve the end he supremely desires, and so to which he earnestly aspires.

The spiritual level of an individual's life conditions the

spiritual significance of every aspect of his life, and so it conditions his interpretation of the religious significance of ritual. A ritual is an instance of magic when an individual believes that it has an efficacy by means of which alone he can accomplish all he desires. It is an element in religious life, however, when it is regarded as a means for clarifying his dependence upon the ultimate reality which he trusts for its dependability.

Men from the earliest historical times have participated in rituals. Whether all of these have a right to enter into the history of religion depends, therefore, not upon their form, but upon their motive, and so upon the attitude of individuals toward them.

3. *The motivation of religious ritual is acknowledging dependence upon an ultimate reality*

The motivation of religious life is to do all that man believes is worthy of himself in acknowledging his dependence upon, and indebtedness to, the reality he trusts for its pre-eminent dependability. An inscription attributed to Darius I, for example, affirms: "A great god is Ahura Mazda, who has created the heaven, and has created man; who has created good things for man." Underlying this inscription is a motivation which underlies every religious act: It is acknowledging man's dependence upon the ultimate reality to which he is indebted for all the goods of life he cherishes. The specific goods for which he is indebted, and for which he acknowledges his dependence, reveal what he regards as most important in his life. Aware that it is "by the favor of Ahura Mazda" that he is "a friend of right," Darius, the king, acknowledged his dependence upon Ahura-Mazda for his ability to rule with wisdom.[13]

Every act in human life is religious when it is an earnest effort in relating oneself to the ultimate reality he reveres for its pre-eminent worthiness to be trusted. Prayer is one such religious act, although its forms may be many. But no act of life is either religious, or a prayer, unless it is a means by which man does what he can to revere the reality upon which he is aware of his final dependence. It is, consequently, a disservice to an understanding of religious life to extend the scope of prayer to include every earnest act or attitude. It is such a disservice, for example, to maintain that "the spirit of prayer" is "primarily a receptive disposition towards everything which can detach me from my self and from my tendency to blind myself to my own failings."[14] The referent of religious prayer is not "everything." It is a very specific reality: It is the one upon which a religious individual finally depends because he trusts it for its pre-eminent dependability. An extension of the scope of prayer to include everything effective in inducing an attitude of detachment is consequently divesting prayer of everything unique to it as an aspect of religious life.

An individual is religious only insofar as he is aware of his final dependence upon an ultimate reality which he trusts as dependable. Insofar, therefore, as an individual's awareness of his final dependence is in any way qualified, to that extent is his religious life also qualified by non-religious ingredients. Turning to a reality for its help is within man's resources, but not the reality from which he seeks his help. This distinction is very clear for a consistently religious individual, but it is not so clear for anyone in whose life there are non-religious tendencies to trust in his own resources, as if they were the source of his most trustworthy help. Hence the margin between a prayer as an element in religious life and a magical device depends on man's point of view toward the role of his prayer.

The referent of religious life is beyond man's own possessions, since the basic conviction of religious life is that man does not possess the means for his own sufficiency. What contributes to man's sufficiency is, therefore, not his own prayer: It is the reality to which he is related by means of his prayer. But it is understandable why prayer is often looked upon as itself efficacious when regarded as a means for relating man to the reality capable of contributing to his life a good which no other reality is capable of doing.

Man's confidence in the final sufficiency of his own possessions is, however, irreligious. Insofar, therefore, as man trusts his prayer as a sufficient means for acquiring a good he supremely desires, he reveals a non-religious confidence in his own acts. A religious individual does not presume to hold within his own control the ultimate source of life and all that sustains it. The only reality he completely trusts for its sufficiency and its unfailing dependability is transcendent of human life, of human possessions, and of the physical world.

Prayer is religious only when it is an acknowledgment of man's final dependence upon the ultimate reality. Hence it is not a presumption to control the ultimate reality. It is rather one of man's means for acknowledging his final helplessness apart from it. But the awareness of helplessness is such a painful experience for an individual who is not consistently religious that he easily develops a confidence in his own possessions and in his own capacities to control the ultimate reality. Insofar, however, as he trusts his own resources for acquiring what he most cherishes, prayer is devoid of religious faith. Religious faith is trust in the ultimate reality. It is not a confidence in man's ability to secure a benefaction apart from it. The very presumption that man can achieve a supremely desired benefit by virtue of any of his own acts or possessions is, therefore, a negation of religious faith.

Any one of man's possessions becomes a magical device when it is regarded as the final means for attaining what he supremely cherishes. A prayer, for example, assumes the status of such a magical device when it is believed to be capable of coercing a supernatural reality to bring about what man cherishes. A belief in a supranatural reality is, therefore, shared both by individuals who trust in magic and by religious individuals who acknowledge their final dependence upon an ultimate reality. One of the most widely articulated utterances on the earth is *O-mi-to-fo,* by which Amitabha, King of the Western Paradise, is addressed. "In time of sickness and loss, in calamity by fire and water, when attacked by robbers, or in the anguish of death, he is the refuge sought."[15] In their urgent need, however, many Tibetans and Chinese trust the expression itself to accomplish for them the good they intend to seek from their deity. Thus they trust one of their possessions in a way which qualifies their dependence upon deity. Such confidence in the name of a deity accounts for the superstitious practice of inscribing it on every type of article associated with what is important in their life, as for example, bracelets worn by children as precaution against disease.

Since it is a world-wide tendency for men to revere certain linguistic expressions as possessing special efficacy, it is difficult, if not impossible, to ascertain which *O-mi-to-fo* is a prayer, and which is a magical formula. A distinction between prayer and magic is preserved by an individual alone who retains his faith that the only reality worthy of his trust is transcendent of human life, of human possessions, and of the physical world. Insofar as he forgets this, the role of his prayer is non-religious. Although *O-mi-to-fo* "is one of the most sacred concepts of the East Asiatic consciousness," it is also one of the most widely used of magical formulae. Buddhist monks greet one another with this expression. "Lay people mumble it, heartily or mechanically, at work and at worship." The fact alone that this expression is "repeated several thousand times a day in the religious processions through corridors and temple halls"[16] does not confer upon it immunity to misuse. The misuse of every element in religious life is possible by non-religious individuals; and is imminent even in religious individuals in moments in which they lose the clarity of their awareness of dependence upon an ultimate reality.

A common representation of Amitabha is guiding the "Ship of Salvation" over the "Sea of Sorrows" toward the shores of the Western Paradise. Some people in this pictorial representation are portrayed as passengers securely protected in the boat piloted by Amitabha. Others are portrayed as struggling to be saved—stretching out their hands toward the sail upon which is written *Mi-to*, the short form of *O-mi-to-fo*. Reaching toward a sail on which is written the abbreviated name of deity is thus one pathetic manifestation of the tragic plight of human life; profoundly in need of help, and yet, wavering in its trust of a completely dependable source of help. The helplessness of human life in an hour of crisis enables one to understand why anything to which a person can cling may become a means to sustain his courage and to give him confidence.

For one who believes in the special efficacy of language, the name of deity is regarded as a possession for subordinating the power of deity to man's own control. This trust in language is not an outgrowth of religious faith. It is rather a constant threat to religious faith, since it is a constant temptation of men to trust in their own possessions as sufficient means for attaining ends which they supremely desire. Trust in the special efficacy of language is, therefore, worldwide; and wherever men are religious, they live in a context in which the superstitious awe for the magical efficacy of language is also present. This fact accounts for the intrusion of some superstition into religious life, and for the conversion of some prayers into magical formulae.

One aspiration of religious life is to enter into a new order of living by virtue of man's orientation to the ultimate source of all worthy goods. A Zoroastrian prayer is "O Mazda, first of all things I will pray for the works of the holy spirit."[17] One of the aspirations in Mithraism, for example, is the desire to be "born anew in the Spirit," and "the whole of its ritual was deliberately planned to explain this goal and to indicate the steps by which the individual became one with his Father."[18] What constitutes the religious nature of Mithraism is what also constitutes the religious nature of Christian life. It is an orientation to the divine reality, worshiped as the one and only source from which man presumes to derive whatever is of utmost worth in his life.

The motivation of all religious life is to become oriented to the ultimate reality which man esteems as pre-eminently worthy of his worship. Included in this motivation is his desire to express his indebtedness to this reality by means of some sacrifice. The flute for the worhipers of Krishna is a symbol of the "call of the Infinite to leave all"; and to help men achieve this, Ramanuja, the religious teacher of the twelfth century A.D., founded seven hundred monasteries. A history of monasticism is, therefore, an important part of the history of religious life, and it justifiably constitutes a considerable part not only of the history of the Christian Church, but also of the history of Buddhism, of Taoism, and of Hinduism. The earnest desire of devout religious life to surrender whatever decreases its awareness of its total dependence upon the divine ultimate accounts for sacrifice in the history of all religions. Primitive men pour their own blood upon the earth as a sacrifice to the reality they worship for its ultimate control over the fertility of the soil. Buddhist pilgrims kneel "every third or tenth step" on their way to a sacred shrine. The Emperors of China placed offerings of silk on the altar to Heaven with the prayer that they "may rise toward the distant blue on the wings of the mighty flames and be received."[19] The people of Seville enthrone the Macarena Virgin in jewels, and cherish the privilege of carrying her image for hours, although each palanquin, laden with gold and gems, weighs in excess of two tons. All religious life is aware of its dependence upon an ultimate reality, and what it does to acknowledge this dependence constitutes the peculiar features of its sacrifice.

It would certainly be a mistake always to correlate what an individual sacrifices with a religious motivation, since there are motives for sacrifice which are not religious. It would likewise be a mistake to look upon sacrifice as extrinsic to religious life. Since religious life is an acknowledgment of man's dependence upon an ultimate reality, some type of sacrifice or self-surrender is integral to it. Hinayana Buddhists, for example, consider it their responsibility to relinquish every possession which in any way deflects them from the eradication of *karma,* and from "the setting free of the soul from its involvement"; and for the attainment of this, they believe that "the most rigorous regulation of all thinking and doing" is indispensable.

Every sound principle of life can be carried to extremes, and one of the problems with which religious life is confronted is the specific application of the sound principle of sacrifice. One of the strictest traditions among Buddhist monasteries goes to the extreme of maintaining that "a monk who has any property, even clothes, cannot reach Nirvana."[20] Thus pressing a worthy principle to an extreme conclusion becomes the specific practice of the Digambaras, the "sky-clad" Buddhist monks.[21]

The motivation for sacrifice or renunciation is not necessarily religious. An exhortation in the Dhammapada is "Seek not that which is dear . . . There are no chains for them who hold nothing dear or not dear."[22] This exhortation to renunciation is not religious simply because it occurs in religious literature. A non-religious moralist, such as Epicurus, might also propose it. What makes sacrifice or renunciation specifically religious is its motivation. It is religious only when it expresses man's acknowledgment of his indebtedness to an ultimate reality. Thus even sacrifice of the most extreme form is not religious unless its motivation is religious, which is to acknowledge man's supreme indebtedness to an ultimate reality for all that he cherishes. What men consider worthy of cherishing is revealed in what they regard as compatible with their religious life, and so with all they do for a specific religious motivation. The Pythagorean brotherhood, for example, required a disciple to burn his property; to remain in silence sometimes three years, sometimes five years, and to study; and according to one account, to do so "in rooms underneath the earth."[23]

4. *A universal tendency in religious life is to depend upon symbols*

Any object is religiously significant when it is a means by which man is referred to a reality he trusts for its ultimate dependability. One type of such means is ritual. But after a ritual has acquired religious significance by virtue of its symbolic role, men commonly trust it as if it were the reality of pre-eminent importance in their religious life.

A trust which men place in human possessions is the origin of magic. The origin of religious life, on the other hand, is a trust which men direct to a reality transcendent of human possessions. Hence every ritual in religious life is subject to perversion by the attitude of individuals who center their trust upon a reality other than the Ultimate. The same ritual may, therefore, perform a religious role for one individual, and a magical role for another. A sacrament, according to Cyprian, Bishop of Carthage, is alone effective when "by prayer" man "merits for himself the mercy of God." A sacrament, according to Tertullian, a contemporary Father of the Church, is itself a sufficient means for salvation.[24] Thus the difference between the views of Cyprian and Tertullian is not merely a matter of emphasis: It is rather a radical difference in their interpretation of the role of sacraments.

The religious significance of a ritual is its function in orienting men to an ultimate reality pre-eminently worthy of their trust. According to religious faith, this reality is not within man's life and the physical world. It is other than both. Hence a ritual which is trusted for its sufficiency, independent of its symbolic function, is not an element in religious life. This distinction between a magical device and a religiously significant ritual is perfectly clear as a matter of definition. But the distinction is not equally clear in every religious life in which ritual is an ingredient. The solemn chant of the Kangaroo Men before their totem may, for example, be an element in a religious ritual, or in a magical ceremony. When it is a means for acknowledging their final dependence upon the ultimate determiner of the availability of their food, it is an element in a religious ritual. When it is trusted for its own effectiveness independently of any other reality, it is a magical device. Thus some individuals who participate in a ritual may trust the ritual, whereas others may trust a reality transcendent of the ritual to which it refers. A ritual is religiously significant insofar as an individual regards it as his most worthy way of acknowledging his dependence upon the reality he trusts above every other reality. Its religious significance, in distinction to its magical role, however, cannot be ascertained with accuracy by an anthropologist or a philosopher.

The borderline of magic and religion is not even clear for many who participate in ritual. One hundred and thirty conspirators were once hung in the Palazzo Communale, whereupon "thirty-five altars were erected in the square, and for three days mass was performed and processions held to take away the curse which rested on the spot."[25] It would be a mistake to assume that this attempt to remove a presumed curse was motivated by religious faith just because altars were used and masses were performed. Insofar as altars and masses were employed as instruments for accomplishing a supremely desired end, their use may have been religiously motivated, or it may have been motivated without a shred of religious faith.

Man's confidence in a ritual as his own possession converts a ritual into a magical device, and in this conversion, religious faith is displaced by another type of confidence. A mass which begins at sunset and continues into the night is, for example, a common ritual among Mahayana Buddhists. The underlying concern of this ritual is an interest in the welfare of the soul of the deceased. Although the concern underlying the ritual is worthy, what is not equally worthy is the confidence that "the more such masses one can afford, the more certain he can be that the dead will come through well."[26] A confidence in what man himself possesses and can do is characteristic of all superstitious trust in magical devices. Confident in his possession of the means for attaining ends he supremely desires, one slips into the arrogant attitude of all who trust in their own possessions as sufficient for the fulfillment of all their needs. An attitude such as this easily irradiates throughout human life, thus accounting for the precarious borderline between magic and religion.

No matter how worthy an end may be that an individual desires as the fulfillment of his most ardent wish, its attainment may tempt him into trusting a reality which he himself is clearly aware is not the ultimate reality. An impatience to achieve an objective without delay accounts in part for the haste with which many people resort to short cuts in their life. Magic is one such short cut by which individuals presume to bypass their dependence upon a reality which is not one of their possessions. A Pure Land Buddhist, for example, desires to enter into the Western Paradise, and to achieve this he believes that he "must do 1,300 good deeds," whereas if he wants to become an "immortal on earth" he "must do only 300 good deeds."[27] The very distinction between the efficacy of one number of human acts and another number expresses a point of view common to a superstitious confidence in magic, as well as to a casuistic confidence in the externals of religion. Man's presumption that he has the formula by which he can enter into an eternal paradise and that he has the capacities to attain this end without depending upon a reality transcendent of himself and his possessions is a type of confidence which underlies all magic. The worthy goal of an eternal life is thus easily converted into an adjunct of superstition by virtue of man's arrogance in presuming that he is the final determiner in the attainment of ends he supremely cherishes.

This confidence may be expressed through any means. Hence the means which a religious individual regards with utmost reverence may also be blighted by this arrogant presumption. Some French peasants, for example, believe in the special efficacy of a "Mass of the Holy Spirit," which they presume can be performed by priests with such skill that God is "forced to grant whatever is asked of Him . . . however rash and importunate might be the petition."[28]

There is nothing in human life which cannot be blighted by the insolence of man, and there is nothing in religion so sacred that it is exempt from his blasphemy. It is a universal temptation for man to presume that he is not ultimately dependent, and wherever this impertinence is not eradicated from his life, he can never be consistently religious. His religion will consist at most in the brief moments in which he acknowledges his dependence. But when his acknowledgment of dependence is only an episode, and is not a fundamental conviction of his life, he is constantly tempted to trust his possessions for the attainment of ends he desires, without subordinating himelf to a reality upon which he is finally dependent.

It was, for example, common for the ancient Egyptians to presume that they could control the gods by devices they themselves possessed. Presuming such control, the very significance of the gods for them was an accommodation to their insolence. Insolent enough to presume that they were in final control of the means for attaining what they most cherished, they rationalized their confidence in magic in their concepts of the nature of gods. Believing that gods rule the world by magic, and believing that magic is "primarily the power of the gods," they presumed that "by learning and understanding the power of the gods" they could control even them. This phase of Egyptian life is, however, not a chapter in the history of religion. It is a chapter rather in the history of magic, which is a record of the folly of men to presume that they are in final control of the means for attaining what they most cherish.

In the case of some of the ancient Egyptian practices, "it is often difficult to know where magic ends and religion begins."[29] But this perplexity is not confined to an interpretation of the motives of the ancient Egyptians. Every element of religious life may be distorted into a non-religious role, which is a result of a non-religious desecration of a means capable of performing a worthy function in religious life. Insofar as man presumes to possess the means adequate for an attainment of all that he desires, without in any way acknowledging that his attainment of such ends is qualified by his dependence upon an ultimate reality, his point of view, and so his life, is not religious. The distinction between religious life and non-religious life is, therefore, not in overt acts. It is in man's attitude toward what he does and toward what he possesses.

Magic has its origin in human life not only by virtue of man's ignorance of cause and effect, although this explanation is very common. An individual who trusts in the efficacy of a means he possesses to have influence upon the events of utmost importance in his life is indeed ignorant both of the nature of such a means, and also of the nature of his life. The use of an oracle for acquiring a knowledge of future events is one instance of such ignorance. But in addition to ignorance, it is also an instance of incredible arrogance to presume that by man's own devices he can predict future occurrences, and so can penetrate beyond the limits of a present. Man's acknowledgment that he is confronted by an impenetrable wall, beyond which he cannot see, is a trial for his arrogance. Unwilling fully to admit his limited status, he presumes to manipulate trinkets he possesses for the high purpose of reading the future. Thus every act of divination by which he presumes the sufficiency of his own means for claiming knowledge of future events is an instance of an impertinence.

Any trust in the sufficiency of man's abilities or possessions apart from his dependence upon a reality transcendent of them is a compromising of religious faith, and to the extent that such a trust irradiates throughout one's life, religious faith is made impossible. It was a customary practice for the ancient Egyptians, for example, to bury with the dead a number of little figures called *ushabtiu* "whose duty was to answer for their client during the trial of judgment."[30] One thus sees in this practice, the intermixture of a religious belief and a superstitious trust in magic. An acknowledgment that his life is under scrutiny of a judgment other than his own is an expression of a profound moral consciousness. But the painful realization that the record of his life must be subject to a judgment other than his own accounts for his desire to reduce his helplessness and his dependence. Believing, therefore, that the *ushabtiu* could qualify his total helplessness, he was tempted to trust what is not the ultimate reality. The *ushabtiu* were his artifacts. No Egyptian was ever so ignorant that he was unaware of the source of his own artifacts. But many, regardless of their intelligence, were tempted to trust them as a means by which they could become less than totally dependent.

It is painful for an individual who is not consistently religious to acknowledge that he is ultimately helpless, and that there is nothing which he possesses or can control, by virtue of his skill or his wealth, which can diminish his ultimate dependence. Hence the painful character of this realization underlies what men do to reduce the completeness of their dependence. Such effort is expressed in every aspect of human life, irradiating even into religion. Thus it is not surprising that religious rituals are subject to a non-religious interpretation, and so to a non-religious use. Even the philosophically brilliant Duns Scotus defended the interpretation of the Lord's Supper as a "covenant (in which) the Lord has obligated himself to . . . give grace to him who receives the sacrament." Thus the intelligence of this philosopher, which is very considerable, was not a safeguard against interpreting the role of a sacrament from the point of view of the presumption that God's grace can be coerced by what man himself does. Failing to distinguish between a sacrament as a means for receiving divine grace, and a sacrament as itself the sufficient means for acquiring it, he attributed to man the capacity of holding within his own possession the ultimate source of supreme benediction. Such a concession to pride is a repudiation of religious faith, and is a desecration of a religious sacrament. Yet this desecration of a sacrament by virtue of man's arrogance became a dominant practice in the Christian Church during the later Middle Ages.[31]

The borderline between magic and religion is, therefore, one of the precarious grounds over which human life must struggle if it is to attain the clarity of a religious consciousness of man's unqualified dependence upon an ultimate reality. Even the ritual of religious institutions is subject to a non-religious interpretation by individuals who are not consistently religious in their point of view, and so in their faith. A non-religious point of view is not peculiar to individuals obviously outside the membership of a religious institution. Individuals within a religious institution are equally capable of a non-religious interpretation of the very ritual whose role in religious life is specifically religious. It is difficult, for example, to ascertain where Ignatius, martyr Bishop of Antioch, placed the emphasis in interpreting the bread of the Sacrament as "the medicine of immortality," and as "an antidote that we might not die, but live in Jesus Christ forever."[32] The emphasis is religious if it is upon Jesus Christ in Whom man enters into an eternal life. But it is an expression of superstitious trust in man's possessions if the emphasis is upon the bread as "an antidote that we might not die." It is likely that Ignatius was guilty of misusing a metaphor in emphasizing the indispensability of the sacrament as an aspect of Christian faith, and in this case, his interpretation of the role of the bread in the sacrament is only defectively expressed. But this charity toward Ignatius does not extend to Abelard, because Abelard's interpretation of the role of the sacrament in Christian life is not stated by means of a metaphor. He specifically declares that "so long as the form (*species*) of the bread and wine is retained, the sacrament continues." Thus in confusing the symbol of a religious sacrament with the ultimate source of help to which religious life turns, he maintained that the sacrament possesses significance for religious life by virtue solely of its "form." Notwithstanding the philosophical accomplishments of Abelard, which are many, his interpretation of the nature of a sacrament differs in no essential way from the irreligious point of view of all who trust in their own possessions.

The precarious margin between the religious role of a sacrament and its non-religious role is clearly illustrated in what the advocates of Abelard's theory concluded about the independent efficacy of the Elements: They "did not even shrink from the conclusion, that if a dog or a mouse should eat the *hostia,* the substance of Christ would remain in it." Whether this conclusion is an instance of naive faith, or of blasphemy—of which sophisticated intelligence is all too capable—is not within the scope of this study to decide. But it is within its scope to point out how precarious it is even to articulate an interpretation of the role of the sacraments lest one emphasize a point of view which he does not intend to emphasize. According to Eugene IV, for example, the sacraments "both contain grace and confer it upon those worthily receiving them."[33] No criticism may be made of the interpretation as stated, when the emphasis is upon the role of the sacrament as contingent upon the worthiness of an individual to receive it. But when a sacrament is construed as itself the means of grace, apart from its role as a religious rite, it is no longer a sacrament. The conversion of a rite of the Church from a sacrament into a magical device is thus a fearful alternative with which every individual is confronted who accepts a sacrament from the ministry of the Church. The worthiness of a sacrament, as well as every other symbol, to be included in religious life must, therefore, always be measured by its function in referring man to the ultimate reality upon which alone he is finally dependent, and upon which his trust is supremely justified.

REFERENCES

Chapter I

1. Marcel, G., *The Mystery of Being*, vol. II, "Faith and Reality," p. 122, Trans. René Hague, Regnery, Chicago, 1951.
2. Reichelt, K. L., *Religion in Chinese Garment*, p. 58, Trans. J. Tetlie, Philosophical Library, N.Y., 1951.
3. Suzuki, D. T., *An Introduction to Zen Buddhism*, p. 124; 122, Philosophical Library, N.Y., 1949.
4. *The Nature of Religion*, p. 13, Trans. T. Menzel and D. S. Robinson, Crowell, N.Y., 1933.
5. *Ibid.*, p. 6.
6. *Op. cit.*, p. 69.
7. Wobbermin, G., *op. cit.*, p. 6.
8. *Archeology and the Religion of Israel*, p. 42; 43, Johns Hopkins, Baltimore, 1942.
9. "Religion in Prehistoric Greece," *Forgotten Religions*, ed. V. Ferm, p. 162, 161, Philosophical Library, N.Y., 1950.
10. *The Origins and History of Religions*, p. 144, Philosophical Library N.Y., 1952.
11. Elkins, A. P., "The Religion of the Australian Aborigines." *For. Rel.*, p. 284.
12. *Op. cit.*, p. 147.
13. *Op. cit.*, p. 43.
14. *Ibid.*, p. 264.
15. *Op. cit.*, p. 163.
16. *De Anima* 415b, 26: 416b, 19.

Chapter II

1. Wyman, L. C., "The Religion of the Navaho Indians," *Forgotten Religions*, p. 352; 353.
2. Finegan, J., *The Archeology of World Religions*, p. 51, 61, Princeton University Press, Princeton, 1952.
3. Gaster, T. H., "The Religion of the Canaanites," *For. Rel.*, p. 124.
4. 10; 10: Cf. *Judges* 16; 23: *I Samuel* 5; 2–7.
5. Finegan, J., *op. cit.*, p. 61–62.
6. Murphy, J., *The Origins and History of Religions*, p. 188.
7. Güterbock, H. G., "Hittite Religion," *For. Rel.*, p. 88.

186 REFERENCES

8. Gaster, T. H., *op. cit.*, p. 122.
9. Reichelt, K. L., *Religion in Chinese Garment*, p. 46.
10. Finegan, J., *op. cit.*, p. 130.
11. *Joshua* 15; 10: 15; 7.
12. Mylonas, G. E., "Religion in Prehistoric Greece," *For. Rel.*, p. 152.
13. Elkin, A. P., "The Religion of the Australian Aborigines," *op. cit.*, p. 278.
14. Murphy, J., *op. cit.*, p. 64; 187.
15. *Ibid.*, p. 63; 40; 33; 20; 64.
16. Otto, R., *The Idea of the Holy*, p. 31; 128; 45; 7; 20; 10; 77; 52; Trans. J. W. Harvey, Ninth Impression, 1943, Oxford, N.Y.
17. *Anguttara Nikâya*, V., quoted from Wobbermin, *op. cit.*, p. 165.
18. Giles, H., *Chang Tzŭ, Mystic, Moralist, and Social Reformer*, p. 279, Trans. from the Chinese, 2nd. ed., Kelley and Walsh, Shanghai, 1926.
19. Taraporewala, I. J. S., "Mithraism," *For. Rel.*, p. 214.
20. Mylonas, G. E., "Mystery Religions of Greece," *op. cit.*, p. 174.
21. Wyman L. C., *op. cit.*, p. 360.
22. Murphy, J., *op. cit.*, p. 108.
23. Finegan, J., *op. cit.*, p. 63.
24. *Archeology and the Religion of Israel*, p. 24.
25. *The Christian Faith*, p. 13ff, ed. H. R. Mackintosh and S. S. Stewart, Clark, Edinburgh, 1928.

Chapter III

1. Wobbermin, G., *The Nature of Religion*, p. 151; 15.
2. *Metaphysics* 993a, 10.
3. H. H. Risley declares that "the shifting and shadowy company of unknown powers or tendencies making for evil rather than for good, which reside in the primeval forest, in the crumbling hills, in the rushing river, in the spreading tree, which gives its spring to the tiger, its venom to the snake" is the "sort of power" in which the jungle tribes of Chutia Nagpur believe. *The People of India*, p. 224, 2d. ed., Thackery, London, 1915.
4. Smith, E. W., *The Religion of Lower Races as Illustrated by the African Bantu*, p. 10, Macmillan, N.Y., 1923. ("The African . . . does not make a creed of his belief in this energy; he acts upon it. His religion consists very largely in getting this power

REFERENCES

to work for his benefit and in avoiding that which would bring him into violent and harmful contact with it.")

5. Finegan, J., *Archeology of World Religions*, p. 13.
6. Gaster, T. H., "The Religion of the Canaanites," *For. Rel.*, p. 120.
7. Murphy, J., *The Origins and History of Religions*, p. 72.
8. Waley, A., *The Way and Its Power*, p. 31–2, Houghton Mifflin, Boston, 1935.
9. Ackerman, P., *Ritual Bronzes of Ancient China*, 74; 81, Dryden, N.Y., 1945.
10. Murphy, J., *op. cit.*, p. 254.
11. In Saiva shrines "the main sanctum . . . almost invariably contains the supreme emblem of the father-god, the Siva linga. That is the chief object of veneration . . . The main idea underlying the Siva linga in its most primitive aspect was undoubtedly phallic." Banerjea, J. N., "The Hindu Concept of God," p. 64, *The Religion of the Hindu*, ed. K. W. Morgan, Ronald, N.Y., 1953.
12. Murphy, J., *op. cit.*, p. 210.
13. Gaster, T. H., *op. cit.*, p. 121–2.
14. Willoughby, W. C., *Nature-Worship and Taboo*, p. 120 ff, Hartford, 1932. Cf. also Gilmore, G. W., *Animism*, p. 99 ("By the inhabitants of New Guinea, spirits . . . are supposed to inhabit any place with unusual physical characteristics—water-fall, pool, queer-shaped rock, or the like.") Boston, 1919.
15. Finegan, J., *op. cit.*, p. 202.
16. Tylor defines animism as a "development (which) includes the belief in souls and in a future state, in controlling deities and subordinate spirits." *Primitive Culture*, p. 427, Third American ed. from the second English ed., Holt, N.Y., 1889.
17. *Op. cit.*, p. 121.
18. Whitehead, H., *The Village Gods of South India*, p. 23, Oxford, London, 1921.
19. Aristotle, *De Anima* 405a, 19.
20. Codrington, R. H., *The Melanesians, Studies in Their Anthropology and Folklore*, p. 118, n. 1, Oxford, London, 1891.
21. *Metaphysic* 1074b, 1.

Chapter IV

1. Kramer, S. N., "Sumerian Religion," *Forgotten Religions*, p. 56.
2. Taraporewala, I. J. S., "Mithraism," *ibid.*, p. 205.
3. *Mundaka-Upanishad* 11, ii, 2. (Cf. Chatterjee, S. C., "Hindu

Religious Thought," *The Religion of the Hindus,* p. 218 for interpretation of Brahman; and Banerjia, J. N., "The Hindu Concept of God," p. 74, for distinction of Brahman from Brahma, the Creator.)

4. *Textbook of the History of Doctrines,* vol. 1, p. 39, Lutheran Publication Society, Philadelphia, 1905. (Reference to *II Cor.* 3; 17)

5. Udāna VIII, 3. quoted from Wobbermin, G., *op. cit.,* p. 142.

6. Murphy, J., *op. cit.,* p. 347.

7. Waley, A., *The Way and Its Power,* p. 141; 174, Unwin and Allen, London, 1935.

8. Moule, A. C., *Christians in China Before the Year 1550,* p. 36, Macmillan, N.Y., 1930.

9. Reichelt, K. L., *Religion in Chinese Garment,* p. 45, trans. Joseph Tetlie, Philosophical Library, 1951.

10. Yasna 44: 3–5 from Moulton J.H., *Early Religious Poetry of Persia,* Cambridge, 1911.

11. Aristotle, *Metaphysics,* 983b, 26.

12. Nahm, M., *Selections from Early Greek Philosophers,* p. 63, Crofts, N.Y. 1940.

13. Aristotle, *De Anima* 411a, 8.

14. Plato, *Theatetus* 183 E.

15. "Concerning Truth," 98, Nahm, M., *op. cit.,* p. 117.

16. *Fragments* 36, Nahm, M., *ibid.,* p. 91.

17. *Ibid.,* p. 90, *Fragments* 19.

18. Taittirīya Upanishad iii, quoted from Schweitzer, A., *Indian Thought and its Development,* p. 35, trans., Mrs. C. E. B. Russell, Holt, N.Y., 1936.

19. *Op. cit.,* p. 117.

20. *Lives of Eminent Philosophers,* vol. 11, Bk. IX, 8, trans., R. D. Hicks, Loeb Classical Library, 1931.

21. Aristotle, *Metaphysics,* 985b, 26.

22. *Fragments* 6, quoted from Nahm, M., *op. cit.,* p. 150.

23. Cf. Bradley, F. H., *Appearance and Reality,* (. . . "Short of the Absolute, God cannot rest, and having reached that goal, he is lost and religion with him.") p. 447, Allen and Unwin, London, 1925.

24. Finegan, J., *op. cit.,* p. 61.

25. Kramer, S. N., "Sumerian Religion," *For. Rel.,* p. 55.

26. Seeberg, R., *op. cit.,* p. 119.

27. *John I,* 9.

28. Seeberg, R., *op cit.,* p. 208.

29. *Ibid.,* p. 244.

30. *Ibid.*, p. 217.
31. *Ibid.*, p. 226.
32. *Ibid.*, p. 224.
33. *Ibid.*, p. 125.
34. *Ibid.*, p. 223.
35. *Ibid.*, p. 225.
36. *Ibid.*, p. 223.
37. *Ibid.*, p. 167.
38. *Ibid.*, p. 166.
39. *Ibid.*, p. 173.
40. *Ibid.*, p. 205.
41. *Ibid.*, p. 229.
42. *Ibid.*, p. 236.
43. Sayce, A. H.,*The Religions of Ancient Egypt and Babylonia*, p. 267, Scribners, N.Y., 1899.
44. Güterbock, H. G., "Hittite Religion," *For. Rel.*, p. 88.
45. Seeberg, R., *op. cit.*, p. 230.
46. Güterbock, H. G., *op. cit.*, p. 91.
47. Griswold, H. D., *The Religion of the Rigveda*, p. 175–6, Oxford, London, 1923.
48. *Op. cit.*, p. 90.
49. Güterbock, H. G., *op. cit.*, p. 88.
50. "Religion in Prehistoric Greece," *For. Rel.*, p. 164.
51. Seeberg, R., *op. cit.*, p. 166.
52. *Ibid.*, p. 203.
53. *Ibid.*, p. 168.
54. *Ibid.*, p. 220.
55. *Ibid.*, p. 208.
56. *Ibid.*, p. 228.
57. *On the Trinity* V, 9.

Chapter V

1. Ackerman, P., *Ritual Bronzes of Ancient China*, p. 79.
2. Reichelt, K. L., *Religion in Chinese Garment*, p. 59.
3. *Fragments* Bk. III, 344, quoted from Nahm, M., *op. cit.*, p. 139.
4. *Basic Writings of Saint Thomas Aquinas*, vol. 1, p. 94, (Q. XXII, Art., II) ed. Anton C. Pegis, Random House, N.Y., 1945.
5. *Ibid.*, p. 97, (Q. XII, Art. IV).
6. *Ibid.*, p. 121, (Q. XIII, Art. V).
7. *Metaphysics* 1074b. 4.
8. Professor Urban says "the true path to reality consists, not in denying but in perfecting and completing the principles of ex-

pression and symbolism," *Language and Reality*, p. 451, Allen and Unwin, London, 1939.

9. As H. R. Mackintosh points out, "it is not merely the concept of Personality that (Schleiermacher) judged unfitted to the Divine Nature, but any objective determination claiming to be valid of God as He really is, or setting up to be more than an imaginative symbol." *Types of Modern Theology*, p. 83, Nisbet, London, 1947.

10. Güterbock, H. G., "Hittite Religion," *Forgotten Religions*, p. 98.

11. Reichelt, K. L., *op. cit.*, p. 17.

12. Finegan, J., *Archeology of World Religions*, p. 89.

13. *Fragments of Heraclitus* 58, quoted from Nahm, M., *op. cit.*, p. 92.

14. Finegan, J., *op. cit.*, p. 178. Cf. "The Hymn to the Supreme Being—The Purusha-sūkta," *The Religion of the Hindus*, p. 280: "Covering the world all around, He (the Supreme Being) yet exceeded it by a span. All this is the Supreme Being, what is past and what is in the future; He is the Lord of immortality as well as of that which grows by food (mortal creatures)."

15. Suzuki, D. T., *An Introduction to Zen Buddhism*, p. 45.

16. *De Anima* 420b, 20.

17. Murphy, J., *The Origins and History of Religions*, p. 132.

18. *Cratylus* 397 D, trans. H. N. Fowler, Loeb Classical Library.

19. W. Washburn Hopkins, however, maintains that "The chief deities in this Chinese system are first Heaven and all its parts, Sun, Moon, Stars, the five planets, especially the twenty-eight signs of the lunar zodiac and certain constellations, such as the Great Bear. Second, the Earth and all its parts, mountains, rivers, soil, grain, earthquakes, drought . . ." *The History of Religions*, p. 244, Macmillan, N.Y., 1918.

20. Fitzgerald, C. P., *China*, 341, Cresset, London, 1935.

21. Reichelt, K. L., *op. cit.*, p. 33.

22. Finegan, J., *op. cit.*, p. 343.

23. *Op. cit.*, p. 79.

24. Mylonas, G. E., "Religion in Prehistoric Greece," *For. Rel.*, p. 161; 150; 152.

25. "Hittite Religion," *For. Rel.*, p. 86.

26. Reichelt, K. L., *op. cit.*, p. 10.

27. *Isaiah* XLV, 3: XVII, 6, 7.

28. Reichelt, K. L., *op. cit.*, p. 136.

29. Mylonas, G. E., *op. cit.*, p. 160.

30. *Isaiah* XLII, 8.

31. Finegan, J., *op. cit.*, p. 58.

REFERENCES

32. Murphy, J., *op. cit.*, p. 81; 266.
33. Gaster, T. H., "The Religion of the Canaanites," *op. cit.*, p. 122.
34. *Op. cit.*, p. 87.

Chapter VI

1. Ackerman, P., *Ritual Bronzes of Ancient China*, p. 69; 70.
2. *Outline of the Religious Literature of India*, p. 6, Oxford, London, 1920.
3. Cf., Elkin, A. P., "The Religion of the Australian Aborigines," *For. Rel.*, p. 276.
4. Cf., Willoughby, W. C., Nature-Worship and Taboo, p. 120ff, Hartford Seminary Press, Hartford, 1932.
5. Fowler, W. W., *The Religious Experience of the Roman People*, p. 78, Macmillan, London, 1911.
6. Gaster, T. H., "The Religion of the Canaanites," *For. Rel.*, p. 118.
7. Elkin, A. P., *op. cit.*, p. 279.
8. Finegan, J., *Archeology of World Religions*, p. 47.
9. Wyman, L. C., "The Religion of the Navaho Indians," *For. Rel.*, p. 347; 353.
10. Finegan, J., *op. cit.*, p. 344.
11. Murphy, J., *The Origins and History of World Religions*, p. 105.
12. *Romans* VI, 4.
13. Finegan, J., *op. cit.*, p. 95.
14. Marcel, G., *The Mystery of Being*, vol. II, p. 105, Regnery, Chicago, 1951.
15. Reichelt, K. L., *op. cit.*, p. 144.
16. *Ibid.*, p. 126.
17. Yasna 28:1, quoted from Moulton, J. H., *Early Zoroastrianism*, p. 344, Williams and Norgate, London. 1913.
18. Taraporewala, I. J. S., "Mithraism," *For. Rel.*, p. 214.
19. Reichelt, K. L., *op. cit.*, p. 46.
20. Finegan, J., *op. cit.*, p., 218.
21. Stevenson, M., *The Heart of Jainism*, p. 12, Oxford, New York, 1915.
22. Verses 210–212, quoted from Wobbermin, G., *The Nature of Religion*, p. 177.
23. Nahm, M., *Selections from Early Greek Philosophers*, p. 80.
24. Seeberg, R., *History of Doctrines*, vol. 1, p. 134.
25. Burckhardt, J., *The Civilization of the Renaissance In Italy*, p. 16, trans. S. G. C. Middlemore, Oxford, N.Y.

26. Reichelt, K., *op. cit.*, p. 65.
27. *Ibid.*, p. 92.
28. Frazer, James, *The Magic Art*, vol. 1, p. 232, Macmillan, London, 1911.
29. Mercer, S. A. B., "The Religion of Ancient Egypt," *For. Rel.*, p. 40; 41.
30. *Ibid.*, p. 36.
31. Seeberg, R., *op. cit.*, vol. 11, p. 127.
32. *Ibid.*, vol. 1, p. 68.
33. *Ibid.*, Vol. II, p. 132; 127.

INDEX

abasement, feeling of, 54
Abelard, 183
Aborigines, Australian, 18, 44
Ackerman, P., 78, 148
adjustment, 42, 66
   religious, 18, 65, 66, 70
Aeschylus, 110
aesthetic, 101
Africa, 74, 88
Agni, 29, 128
Ahura Mazda, 138, 140, 171
Ainus, 7, 8, 28, 29, 63
air, 97, 105, 112, 141
Albright, W. F., 14, 15, 60
Alexander, Bishop of Alexandria, 117, 118, 119
Alexandria, Council of, 121
Algonquins, 74, 159
Allah, 23, 24, 56, 108
altar, 14, 133
Amon-Ra, 146, 151, 165
analysis, philosophical, 68
   psychological, 51
Anaxagoras, 111
Anaximander, 104
Anaximenes, 97, 105, 106
Ancyra, Bishop of, 129
Andaman, 157
Angra Mainyu, 138
animatism, 86, 91
animism, 41, 86, 88, 91
anthropologist, 17, 18, 89
anthropology, 52, 89
anthropomorphism, 134
Antioch, Council of, 122
Anubis, 144
Apache, 95, 143, 155, 168
Apeiron, 104
Aphrodite, 40
Appollinaris, 119, 120
archeologist, 12, 14
Aristotle, 29, 70, 87, 93, 94, 95, 104, 135
Arian, 118, 122, 129
Ariminian, Council of, 112

Arius, 117, 118, 119
artifact, 13, 16, 18, 19, 83
arung quilta, 74, 75
Arunta, 74
Aryans, 36, 40, 141, 156
Asia Minor, 40
assumption, 15, 16, 20, 21, 22, 23, 26
Astarte, 40
Ashtoreth, 40
Athanasius, 118, 129
Atman, 59, 63
Augustine, St., 130, 131
authority, final, 64
   for life, 120
Avesta, 36
Azande, 168

baal, 76, 157
   land of, 34
Babylonian, 40, 114, 126, 128, 130
Balamma, 160
Bantu, 17, 88, 146
banyan, 44
Basilides, 123
Bataks, 143
bealim, 76
behavior, religious, 8
Bel, 127
Beth-Shemesh, 36
birth, 45, 48
Boundless, The, 104
Brahma, 35, 99
Brahman, 76, 77, 78, 99, 141
Brahmaputra, 34, 35
bronzes, Chinese, 133
Buddha, 57, 58, 99, 154
Buddhism, 10, 57, 63, 176
   Hinayana, 58, 64
   Mahayana, 179
   Zen, 3, 141
bull, 82, 158

Canaanite, 34, 76, 82, 114, 157, 167
Cappadocians, 130
Challalamma, 89, 160

INDEX

Chant, Blessing, 31
Chinese, 41, 77, 100, 102, 151, 168
Chou, 100
Christ, 24, 117, 118, 120, 121
Christian, 24, 175
   church, 117, 118, 123, 126, 130, 134, 175, 183
   doctrine, 121
   faith, 117
christology, 120, 122
Chuang Tzu, 147
Chu Hsi, 113
chu lung, 151
classification, 12, 13, 14, 15, 16, 17, 23, 46, 147
Cleanthes, 108
Confucianism, 10, 134, 169
Confucius, 100, 101, 134, 148
Constantinople, 119
contemplation, 61, 147
control, ultimate, 67, 73, 78
controversy, doctrinal, 120, 121
conviction, religious, 69
cosmology, 94, 97
Creator, 117, 130, 134, 153, 155
creed, Nicene, 122
Crete, 15, 128
criteria, 109
crisis, ix, 48
cult, 32, 164
   kachina, 32
   mountain, 149
culture, 23, 38, 45, 46, 66, 86
   ancient, 129
   civilized, 65, 70, 76, 86
   oriental, 99
   primitive, 43, 65, 70, 75, 76, 115
cynicism, 125
Cyprian, 177

Dagan, 32
Darius, 171
definition, 1, 3, 4, 6, 12, 18, 101
   function of, 4
   religion, 7, 18
deity, 126
Demeter, 37
Democritus, 94, 95
dependability, 93, 102
dependence, x, 47, 65, 67
   acknowledgment of, 161
   feeling of, 61, 68, 69

dependence (cont.)
   ultimate, 6, 7, 11, 28, 66, 77, 81, 101
derivation, 106
dingir, 114
destiny, 108
determiner, final, 67, 68, 85
Dhammapada, 176
dharma, 57, 63, 64
Diana, 40
Digambaras, 176
Dionysian, 60
Dionysius of Alexandria, 125
Dionysos, 60
doctrine, 63, 120
dogma, 63
dualism, 41, 88, 139
Duns Scotus, 182
dynamism, 84, 85, 86, 87

Egyptians, 32, 33, 36, 40, 49, 50, 51, 55, 59, 138, 144, 163, 180, 181
Eileithyia, 128
el, 76, 82
elements, four, 104
elim, 76
elohim, 76, 108
Eleusinian, 16
Empedocles, 134
enlightenment, 93, 101, 106
En Shemesh, 36
Ephesus, 40
Epicurus, 2, 177
Eskimo, 166
Eugene IV, 184
Eunomius, 123
Eusebius, 120
Euzoius, 121
experience, aesthetic, 101
   religious, 10, 48, 61, 64, 68, 69, 101

faith, 9, 109
   Christian, 24, 118, 123
   Hebraic, 121
   religious, 10, 11, 77, 91, 93, 94, 97, 102, 103, 113, 114, 120, 122
failure, intellectual, 114
Farquhar, J. N., 164
Fate, 108, 109
fear, 46, 48, 72
feeling, creature, 55
fertility, 36, 128, 145, 157
fields, 37

INDEX

fertility (cont.)
  human, 40
  representation of, 81
  soil, 47, 82
  spirit of, 38, 39
Finegan, J., 128
fire, religious significance, 28
food, dependence upon, 30
  quest, 49
  religious significance of, 5, 7, 26, 27, 28, 29, 49
forces, destructive, 84
Frazer, J., 89
freedom, 57
function, denotative, 84
  magical, 20, 78
  referential, 95
  religious, 20, 80
  sign, 79, 103, 151

Ganges, 35
Gautama, 58, 144
Genesis, 111, 155
God, 108, 112, 118, 120, 121, 124, 130
Godhead, 127
god, healing, 128
  moon, 91
  pearl, 89
  seas, 128
  sky, 98
  soil, 133
  war, 128
  water, 89
Good, Idea of, 115
grace, 184
Greece, 16, 37, 104
Greeks, prehistoric, 37, 55
Guiana, 87, 88
Güterbock, H. G., 128, 150

Hanuman, 156
Heaven, The, 100, 101, 113, 134
  altar of, 102
heavens, 98, 101, 112, 176
hedonism, 2, 66, 67, 68
Heraclitus, 49, 107, 108, 109, 115
Hesiod, 134
Hindu, 59, 60, 61, 63, 76, 78, 99, 130
Hinduism, 35, 36, 141, 156, 175
Hippolytus, 122
Hittites, 33, 43, 44, 127, 128, 130, 139, 150, 158

Homer, 110, 134
homage, 113, 120
  worthy of, 121
homoiousios, 121, 123
homoousios, 121, 123, 125
Hopi, 114
hostia, 184
Hsün Tzu, 101
huen, 139
hylozoism, 90, 91
Hymn to Zeus, 108
hypostasis, 121, 123, 130

idolatry, ix
Ignatius, 183
ignorance, 45, 46, 48, 49, 51, 73
immortality, 183
India, 35, 36, 44, 45, 160, 189
Indian, American, 33
Indra, 156
Indus, 35
inference, 21
information, 67
intelligence, 52, 93
intention, 22
interests, animal, 81
  human, 81, 82
interpretation, 13, 21, 65
  informed, 67
  religious, 9
Ionia, 90, 91, 97
Iran, 40
Isaiah, 56
Isis, 40
Islam, 24, 55, 91
Ishtar, 40, 55
Israel, 60

Jains, 45, 88
James, W., 22
Jehovah, 108
Jesus, 29, 99, 123, 124
judgment, metaphysical, 103
  value, 65

kachinas, 32, 60, 114
Kangaroo, men, 8, 10, 178
Kant, I., 56
karma, 144
knowledge, 67, 103, 115
kovave, 60
kwei, 139

Lao-tzu, 101, 102

life, 90
  Christian, 183
  enlightened, 57
  human, 91, 114
  Law of, 57, 58
  religious, 1, 3, 4, 7, 8, 27, 42, 54, 56, 61, 65, 68, 70, 81, 100, 139
Light, The, 117, 122, 130
  of Life, 125, 133
  of lights, 118
Lithuania, 89, 162
Logos, 108, 109, 111, 115, 118, 122

Magdalenian, 20
magic, 75, 79, 170, 179, 180, 181
mana, 73, 74, 79
manitou, 74
Marcel, M., 39
Marcellus, 129
Marcion, 117
Mariamma, 137
Marett, R. R., 89
Mars, 36
mask, 60, 61
mass, 178
  of the Holy Spirit, 180
Melanesian, 74, 79, 92, 104
Merodach, 127
metaphysic, 51, 65, 93, 94, 95, 96, 97, 103, 104, 105, 109, 112, 114, 148
Milesian, 106
millet, religious significance of, 7, 28, 29
Mind, 111, 112
Minoan-Mycenean, 15, 16, 37, 128, 130
Mithra, 36, 59
Mitra, 36
Mohammed, 23, 24, 102
Moira, 108
Monarchianism, 124, 129
Mongolia, 149
monistic, 112
monotheistic, 92, 112, 121, 130
moon, 78, 79, 91, 111, 112
Mother, Earth, 39, 40, 90
  goddess, 40
  Great, 40
Moses, 150
Moslem, 23, 24
mountains, 148, 152
motion, source, 94
motive, ix, 9, 22, 67, 74, 75, 126

motive (cont.)
  moral, 41
  religious, ix, 6, 41, 43, 53, 67, 68, 104, 106, 108, 120
Murphy, J., 17, 19, 21
Mycenae, Acropolis of, 55
Mylonas, G. E., 15, 16, 19, 22, 129
mythology, 106
mysterious, 45, 46, 48, 49, 52
mystery, 46, 49
mysticism, 99, 144

Navaho, 5, 6, 8, 10, 29, 31, 32, 60, 168
Neolithic, 20, 40
Nestorian, 102
New Guinea, 60
Nicene, 122, 129
Nile, 32, 35, 36
  religious significance of, 33, 49, 151
Nirvana, 57, 58, 64
Nous, 111
numen, 55
numinous, 52, 54, 55, 56

observation, 14, 15, 19
offering, mortuary, 21
  sacrificial, 45
Old Testament, 40
O-mi-to-fo, 173, 174
orenda, 74
Orphic, 168
Osiris, 32, 33, 59, 60, 138
Otto, R., 52, 53, 54, 55, 56, 150
ousia, 121, 123, 130

Palaeolithic, 20, 83
Palestine, 12, 14
pantheon, Babylonian, 40
Papuan, 60
Paradise, Western, 173
Parmenides, 107
Paterfamilias, 167
Paul, St., 40, 99, 170
Persians, 36, 59
Pfleiderer, O., 88
phallicism, 79, 80, 88
Philistines, 32
philosophy, 68, 70, 93, 112
  Greek, 91, 93, 98, 104, 105, 110, 115, 123, 134
  hedonistic, 66
  metaphysical, 111

INDEX

philosophy (cont.)
  moral, 59
  primitive, 85, 90
Phoenicean, 40
pillars, rock, 14, 15
Plato, 107, 110, 111, 115
Plotinus, 99, 113
pluralistic, 114
Plutarch, 144
poh, 139
polydaimonism, 162
Polynesian, 165
polytheism, 91, 105, 106, 130
power, 73, 74, 78
  fertility, 79
  life, 83, 84, 86
  magical, 76
  manifestation of, 85
  Supreme, 100
prayer, 6, 171, 172, 173
  pollen, 31
Praxeas, 124
predicable, 83
premise, basic, 94, 96, 97
  metaphysical, 103
  theological, 130
presupposition, 23, 24, 25
priesthood, 76
primitive, 33, 42, 44, 73, 74, 84, 87
principle, explanatory, 105
  first, 105
prohibition, 46, 72
prophets, 130
protection, 88
Pyrenees, 19
Pythagoras, 110, 144, 177

rain, religious significance of, 33
Ramanuja, 141
reality, ultimate, 6, 38, 65, 66, 67, 76, 78, 95, 97, 98, 103, 112, 113, 135
Receptacle, The, 111
Reichelt, K. L., 154
religion, definition of, 4, 23, 48, 51, 68, 75, 84, 92, 108
  philosophy of, 7, 105
  science of, 7
responsibility, intellectual, 126
reverence, 66, 67, 69, 96, 101, 105, 145, 147
Rig-Veda, 35, 165
rite, ritual, bathing, 45, 75, 76, 77,

rite (cont.)
  165, 167
  corn, 6
  cultic, 12
  Dionysian, 16
  Eleusianian, 16
  initiation, 60
  motives of, 9
  sacrificial, 34
  sand painting, 31
river, religious significance of, 35, 151
Romans, 40, 161
Rome, 37, 119

Sabellius, 127, 129
sacrament, 177, 183, 184
sacrifice, 14, 45, 76
salvation, 57, 58
Samas, 127
sanctuary, 12
Sankara, 141
Sariputta, 58
Schleiermacher, F., 61, 62, 63, 68, 89
science, 45, 47, 84
Scriptures, 105, 118, 123, 130, 141
seals, 12, 13
Seeberg, R., 99, 122
Seleucia, Council of, 123
Semites, 36
Seth, 138
Shang, 100
Shang-ti, 34, 100, 102
Shemash, 36
Shen, 139
sign, 27, 29, 73, 95, 98
significance, 66, 78
  estimate of, 66
  life, 67
  philosophical, 103, 108
  religious, 1, 8, 15, 31, 49, 50, 71, 73, 79, 80, 101, 103, 105, 109, 177
  supreme, 65, 66, 67, 69, 70, 76, 85, 89, 102, 105, 107, 114
Simplicius, 104
Sinai, 150, 151
Sioux, 74
Sirmium, Third Council of, 122
Siva, 156
Socrates, 144
Spinensis, 161
stars, 111
Sterculius, 161

Stone Age, 19, 20
subordination, 66, 91, 112, 117
    final, 78
substance, underlying, 104
Sumerians, 36, 97, 114
Summa Theologica, 134
Sumatra, 143
sun, 35, 36, 43, 91
superstition, 147
Supreme Being, 92
survival, 8, 27, 74
Surya, 156
swastika, 154
symbol, ix, 13, 15, 20, 39, 73, 79, 81, 91, 92, 97, 98, 107, 109, 110, 153, 160
    role of, 16, 76, 77, 78, 92
    theistic, 107
symbolism, x, 47, 73, 80, 91, 98
    history of, 93, 99, 123, 139, 156
    philosophy of, 135

taboos, 45, 48, 165
Tai-chi, 113
Tamil, 137
Tao, 58, 63, 101
Taoism, 58, 101
Taoist, 61, 147
Te, 77
Tersteegen, 42, 99
Tertullian, 177
Thales, 90, 104, 105
Theodoret, 123
theology, 70, 123, 128
theory, reality of, 71
    value, 71
Thomas, St., 134
Thoth, 144
Tien, 100, 101, 102, 113
Timaeus, 111
totemism, 17, 32, 168
transcendent, 42, 65, 66, 69, 70, 75, 94, 96, 97, 134
Trinity, The, 130
trustworthy, 115, 118
Tylor, E., 88

Ultimate, The, 67, 82, 105, 107
understanding, 9, 15, 19, 66, 108
Universe, 63, 64
Unmoved Mover, 94
Upanishads, 59, 60, 61, 109
Ursacius, 122
ushabtiu, 181, 182

Valens, 122
value, 65, 72
Varuna, 98, 141, 146
Vedas, 35, 36, 128
Venus, 40
vessels, mortuary, 20
vitalism, 84, 85, 86
vocabulary, philosophical, 85, 111
    primitive, 84, 85
    religious life, 121

wakanda, 74
water, religious significance of, 32, 90, 91
Way, The, 101, 102
Weather God, 33, 127, 150, 157
wisdom, 93
    of God, 118, 119
Witchetty Grub Eaters, 27
Wobbermin, G., 7, 9, 69, 70, 88
worship, 41, 109, 113, 130
    ancestor, 41
    mode of, 81
worthy, to be revered, 122
    to be worshiped, 121
    supremely, 97
Wundt, W., 88

Yang, 113, 139
Yahweh, 108
Ying, 139

Zen, 141
Zeus, 108, 110
zoomorphism, 154, 159
Zorah, 14
Zoroastrian, 103, 128, 130, 138, 140, 175
Zuñi, 31, 32, 60, 90, 114